SWANS OF THE WORLD

In Nature, History, Myth & Art

A. LINDSAY PRICE

COUNCIL OAK BOOKS ∼ TULSA. OKLAHOMA

Council Oak Publishing Company, Inc.,
Tulsa, OK 74120

Printed in the United States of America
98 97 96 95 94   5 4 3 2 1

ISBN 0-933031-81-5

"Place of the Two Swans Art Show" on page 20
Illustration by Rosemary Wood, Osage

Swan Frightened by a Dog, 1745. Jean-Baptiste Oudry (French, 1686-1755) on page 34
North Carolina Museum of Art, Raleigh
Purchased with funds from the North Carolina Art Society

Manuscript illustration in *The Book of Marco Polo* c. 1400 on page 100
Bodleian Library, Oxford, MS. Bodl. 264, fol. 218r

The Trumpeter Swan, Alexander Pope (American, 1900) on page 132
The Fine Art Museums of San Francisco
Museum purchase through gifts from members of the Boards of Trustees,
The Dxe Young Museum Society and Patrons of Art and Music, Friends of the Museum, and
by exchange, Sir Joseph Duveen

Various interior illustrations and photographs by Alice Price

Cover illustration and book design by Carol Stanton

*A part of the proceeds for this book goes
to the Trumpeter Swan Society*

Library of Congress Cataloging-in-Publication Data

Price, Alice L.
    Swans of the world : in nature, history, myth & art / A. Lindsay
Price.
        p.   cm.
    Includes bibliographical references   (p.   ).
    ISBN 0-933031-85-5 : $26.95
    1. Swans.   2. Trumpeter swan.   3. Swans—Folklore.   4. Swans in
art.   I. Title.
QL696.A52P75   1994
598.4'1 —dc20

                                                      94-34308
                                                         CIP

Table of Contents

PREFACE

As to many, a fascination with waterfowl, particularly swans, came to me as a gift of childhood. The first sight of Mute Swans afloat on a reflecting pool at the entrance to one of those ornate movie palaces of the past is an event which informs my life. I had no idea at age five, nor did my parents who pulled my outstretched hand away from an open bill, that swans exist in the wild, and that I would one day see them there.

Decades later, this early memory rekindled, I began some ten years ago to write down observations as I hunted ponds, lakes, and wetlands for swans. I took a camera along, and photographing swans allowed me to retrieve the incandescent moment of seeing them free to swim or to fly.

On days when I wasn't in the field, I began to collect material and to search familiar library shelves for swan lore. Thus I began to explore not only places where swans are, but to look at their meaning as a fabulous emblem of nature depicted in many cultures.

After witnessing wild Trumpeter Swans, I began to think of a work which would not only embrace a kind of natural history of the world's swans, but would also include, from my side of the border, that timeless zone of poetry and myth where understanding between human and animals has long met. Working within traditions established not only in literature but in the sciences, I set to work on material I hoped would have enough readable content for all who love swans, and enough facts to satisfy a seasoned naturalist of many winters and wetland treks.

Many individuals have helped me in my trek through field and library in search of swans and swan lore. I wish to thank Russell Studebaker and fellow members of the Swan Lake Park Waterfowl Society of the City of Tulsa who have provided me with far-flung gems of information, gathered from their own perambulations to swan sites and from swan literature. Of the many, Al Stacey, State of Oklahoma Wildlife Biologist, comes readily to mind.

If ever there were an eyewitness of swans in our time, it is Sir Peter Scott, an artist and naturalist with credentials in both fields. In these pages, I keep references to Scott in the present with the exception of a final passage noting his death in 1989. I have done so because the vitality of his lifetime work continues right now, carried on by his wife, Lady Philippa Scott; his daughter, Dr. Dafila Scott; and by members of the Wildfowl and Wetlands Trust such as Nigel Hewston who took Russell Studebaker and me on a "walkabout" at Slimbridge.

To the scholars who commented on different sections of the text, anthropologists Garrick and Roberta Bailey, together with opera critic and literary scholar Joseph Kestner, and classicist Mary Linda Yeakey, I give my appreciation.

Thanks to Roswell Van Deusen of Michigan, Janine Kyler and family, the Woodruffs, Carol and John of Oklahoma, all of whom allowed me to view swans which they hosted on their lands.

My appreciation also to the biologists and their colleagues Eileen Docekal, Newfoundland, to Professor Janet Kear, Miss June H. White and Lady Scott of the Wildfowl and Wetlands Trust of England, and to Donna Compton, Madeleine Linck and Laurence Gillette of the Trumpeter Swan Society, Minnesota, for their good advice.

To the Arts and Humanities Council of Tulsa who granted me the Feldman Literary Award, I also wish to express appreciation for support in bringing this work to its final stages.

Finally to friends, writers and the publishers of Council Oak Books: Sally Dennison, Paulette Millichap, and Michael Hightower, together with Carol Stanton, designer. I extend thanks for their sustaining interest in this work. They are genuine *rarae aves*.

MAGIC HOUR

Behold the whiteness of my body

And behold the whiteness, the purity of the sky...

The great white swan was

heard to say:

"I shall be the means by which the little

ones can control the sky.

Behold the whiteness of my body

And behold the whiteness, the purity of

the sky.

I am the person who has made himself

to resemble the sky in purity.

When the little ones make of me the

means by which to control the sky

They shall be able through their life's

journey, to make the god of the upper

region

To lie in purity."

Peace Ceremony of the
Osage Tribe, F. LaFlesche,
"War Ceremony and Peace
Ceremony of the Osage Indians"

"There they are!" Russell shouts. He's holding binoculars to his eyes and with one hand points to the far shore of a little lake appearing suddenly in the distance.

The Jeep Cherokee ahead of us has made a sharp right and is proceeding along another dirt road running parallel to the lake. I peer over the Jeep's flume of white dust, and I can see them too. Three swans on the glittering blue lake.

This is a sight I never once imagined I would see so near my winter home. The three wild Trumpeter Swans have migrated south from over a thousand miles away to alight on this obscure little lake in Northeastern Oklahoma. The fact that anyone alive in 1991 would witness these wild swans is what science writers of my youth would call a "modern miracle."

However, 150 years ago, the sight of the Trumpeter Swans was not such a rare one. Audubon saw hundreds when he traveled down the Mississippi to the mouth of the Arkansas River. The waters of this little manmade lake have been captured from that same tributary of the Mississippi, the Arkansas, which flows just five miles or so away from here, along the territory of the Osage Tribe who once hunted this land. These Native Americans, their numbers in the past decimated like the Trumpeter Swan's, had place names like "Swan Crossing," "Swan Pond," and "The Place of the Swans." To the Osage of Indian Territory the swan was not an uncommon sight, but they venerated this great swan for its might and power, and it was a part of their peace ceremonies and their beginnings in myth.

The Jeep stops before a gate, and Al gets out, a tall, powerful man, taut as a wire, an Oklahoma Wildlife Manager who spotted the migratory Trumpeters on the lake over a week ago.

"I can't promise they'll still be there," Al said over the phone this morning.

"You tell me where and when, and I'll be there," I said. "I'll let Russell know."

I stop the car and Russell is out the door before I can throw the gear into park and pick up my camera. There they really are, feeding as peacefully as our own captive pair on Swan Lake. But unlike Swan Lake's newly mated pair, these swans have a young one, a near yearling, probably hatched last spring.

Russell stares through the binoculars in silent wonder. Then he says, "One of them is wearing an identification collar. It's a female, I think. She's riding lower in the water."

I twist my long-range lens into focus and I see her yellow neck band plainly. There are black letters and a number: 59-NC. That means they're from Hennepin Parks, Minnesota where Trumpeter swans are released into the wild in the hope that they will migrate. And they have migrated. They are among the first Trumpeter Swans known to have done so in over a century.

The collared swan's long neck disappears as it feeds on the bottom of the lake. The yearling also plunges its gray neck down and the third swan, which we take to be the male, stands in shallow water preening, his reflection doubling the effect of whiteness. We can see the narrow salmon-colored line on his lower mandible as he thrusts his black bill into his white feathers. Most certainly Trumpeters.

It is that hour photographers call the Magic Hour when the light of late dusk deepens into magical hues and everything in the landscape seems to say, "Yes." Beyond the feeding swans who are only 500 feet away, the long tan grass of the Oklahoma hillside begins to mellow under a yellow-orange light. On the lake farther out, a line of American Golden Eye Ducks twist the circlets of their golden eyes under the lens of a late sun.

I am photographing the three swans from far away enough not to disturb them. Al and Russell talk quietly in low tones; these Trumpeters have long memories of man and are wary. If they are disturbed by humans they might lift off, their great wingspread taking them aloft as they circle back over us, scanning the landscape for another lake located somewhere far off in the magic distance of another sunset.

 EASON OF THE SWAN

The swan as a mythic and a natural wonder

reaches back with its long neck and probes the very edge

of time where the origins of our consciousness lie.

*U*nder the October twilight the

water

mirrors the still sky:

Upon the brimming water among the

stones

Are nine-and-fifty swans.

Unwearied still, lover by lover,

they paddle in the cold

Companionable streams or climb the air;

Their hearts have not grown old;

Passion or conquest wander where they

will,

Attend upon them still.

"The Wild Swans at Coole"
William Butler Yeats

It is late afternoon, and ducks begin to fly in towards a patch of open water in the city park. Descending along the slanting light of a late afternoon sun, they spread their wings, splay their webbed feet and roll on the wind, canting from side to side as they brake their descent. Skidding along the surface of the water, they join over 100 other waterfowl already feeding on the lake.

On shore, geese are grazing among the grasses. Some are white with black wing-tips; others are gray with long black necks, a handsome white wedge at their throats. There are over forty different species of waterfowl congregating here. All are busy pattering and splashing, diving and dabbling.

Among the feeding number, two large white birds uncoil their long necks, turning their heads as if to listen. Then as if hearing a call, they sidle down the bank to push off. Sailing into the water, they proceed majestically along a lake glittering with reds and yellows of the setting sun. These two birds, larger than all the rest, indeed largest of all waterfowl, are swans. Watching, you may separate them easily from the rest of their group, distinguish them readily from Snow Geese, Canada Geese, Mallard Ducks. And though all these waterfowl are members of the same family, *Anatidae*, the white pair are most definitely swans.

Any of the human beings who approach the lake to watch the birds may recognize this pair at once. Men, women, or children may peer quizzically at the geese and ducks, search hastily through their field guides to name the species of waterfowl, but without turning a page, they know these two are swans.

When we watch swans gliding on still water or on the "cold companionable stream" of W. B. Yeats' poem, all our histories lean over our shoulders. The swan as a mythic and a natural wonder reaches back with its long neck and

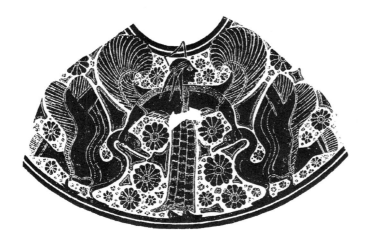

probes the very edge of time where the origins of our consciousness lie.

Its image appears in myth and folklore throughout the world in places where swans may be found, such as in the Bronze Age pin shaped like a swan found by archaeologists in a burial chamber of 1500 B.C., or the Swan of Apollo engraved on Greek coins of the fourth century B.C.

Perceiving this creature within nature, we look with a gaze directed by the stories of our past. Scientists warn us of our subjectivity, and they admonish us against reading into the behavior of animals an anthropocentric (literally " man-centered") message of human traits and purposes — some of them good and some of them bad. We call this inclination anthropomorphism (again "man," but "man changed to animal" or "animal to man").

Human-centered biases are locked into even the dispassionate world of science. Paleontologist Stephen Jay Gould, who knows much of the history of science, calls the problem a "conceptual lock." As an example he points out that "Aristotle and nearly two millennia of successors designated the large bee . . . [the queen] as a king." Knowing ourselves best, we "tend to view other creatures as mirrors of our own constitution and social arrangement" (Gould).

For this tendency to render judgment on animal behavior, a teleology which ascribes human characteristics and ends to the natural world, some animals have suffered a "bad press." Humans have acted upon this judgment, frequently setting out to eradicate certain animal species as their "just deserts."

To the wolf we have given human lust, to the fox our sly cunning. You may run the gamut of deadly sins and find an animal crouching (or slithering) innocently within each category. Equally, however, you may find what we consider our virtues: power and strength soar on the wings of an eagle, and courage flexes in the muscle of a lion. Much of this attitude of the good and the bad has its beginning in myth or folklore, the stories humans have told over and over to explain natural phenomena. These tales have structured our thoughts and survived in our language. Northrop Frye in *Words with Power* points out that we do not rid ourselves of an original idea or metaphor. We know scientifically, for example, that the sun does not "go down" at night or "come up" at dawn, yet we still refer to "sunset" and "sunrise."

These lingering imprints in our language and our stories, still "link us to the natural world," says Frye. Thus myths survive into our modern world. The most advanced sciences may sometimes turn to them as a shorthand to express some complex thoughts and technologies: the Apollo spacecraft project to the moon is a good example, an allusion to the god Apollo and his chariot of swans.

Thus, classical myths have survived in a culture primarily Judeo-Christian which has been distinctly opposed to "pagan gods." Frye explains this survival by pointing out that in early Christian times it gradually "dawned on the poets that 'gods' were not really in competition with the one God of a monotheistic religion, but had much more in common with human beings themselves." A myth, therefore, according to Frye, is "a concentration of the primary concerns that human beings share with animals and even plants."

One such myth, a source of poets and artists since classical Greek times, is that of the sky-god Zeus, ruler of the gods, who transforms himself into many forms at will. He becomes a bull, a cloud, a shower of gold, and when he desires

"Leda and the Swan" (Zeus)
Camarina, didrachm
circa 410 B.C.
Nelson Bunker Hunt Collection

Leda, a mortal and a king's wife, Zeus appears on earth as a swan "of dazzling whiteness" to mate with her. Their union produces two children. And since Leda lay with the King that same night, she bears a total of four off-spring who are twinned in different versions of the story. In one version two of the children, Castor and Clytemnestra, are from her mortal husband, King Tyndarus, and in this version the two descended from Zeus are Pollux and Helen, whose beauty is the excuse for the Trojan War. But no matter the configuration of the children's paternity, the association with the swan and the polarities of love and war are made.

The link of swan and god was extended to Zeus's son, the god Apollo. Consequently, for the Greeks and later the Romans the swan was a sacred bird, a creature sharing not only godlike beauty but warlike power as well. The great Roman, Caesar Augustus, took the swan for his family emblem, it is said, when he overcame Mark Antony at the Battle of Actium.

Another aspect of the swan in myth was the power to prophesy. When Apollo slew the Python at the temple of the oracle, he gained prophetic power. The swan, his sacred bird, was honored to draw his chariot of the sun across the sky to the land behind the north wind and back again, an association with the swan's natural migrations.

The most noted example of the swan's mythic powers as a creature endowed with prophecy, and therefore a kind of spiritual being, is in the writings of Greek philosopher Plato when he reported the great Socrates' last words before death. Socrates compared himself to the swan, saying that the swan, because it was sacred to Apollo, "sings joyfully before its death," for the bird more than any other could "see into an afterlife with the god it served."

Two French 19th century postcards from a sequence of cards telling the story of Leda and the Swan. Courtesy of *James Joyce Quarterly*.

The swan as a transformed being of the celestials knows no particular gender in myth, possibly because the swan's coloration is the same in both sexes. In Greek and Roman stories we find the swan representing the masculine in Zeus and Apollo and in the four persons called "Cycnus." The word "Cycnus" derived from a Greek word is the word from which we get "cygnet," the name of the swan young. The Latin *Cygnus*, the name of the species, is still used in modern biological classification.

The most enduring of the four different men called Cycnus, all eventually transformed into swans, is the one in Ovid's *Metamorphoses*. Phaethon, son of Apollo, was killed when he was permitted by his father to drive the chariot of the sun and lost control thus setting the world on fire. Grandfather Zeus was so angered that he zapped his reckless driver grandson with a lightning bolt, setting him afire and casting him into the sea. Cycnus, Phaethon's friend, grieved for Phaethon, first searching for him in the depths of the waters. *Bullfinch's Mythology* holds that his search is linked with the swan's habit of up-ending or "tipping-up" to search with its long neck for food on the bottom of a pond.

Zeus relented somewhat, and pitying the grieving Cycnus, he set him among the stars. Cycnus became the constellation of the Swan, Cygnus, wheeling above us, visible in the dark of night. The constellation, also called the Northern Cross, is a bearing for mariners and linked to the swan as a sailor's favorable omen, an omen surviving to modern times.

One major text of the world, on the other hand, has not presented the swan as sacred or even as a favorable animal. Listed in Deuteronomy of the Bible, the swan is called one of the "unclean" birds which "ye shall not eat."

Roy Pinney in *The Animals in the Bible* points out that this unfavorable aspect of the swan may have come from a mistranslation of the Hebrew word *tinshemeth*. Some editions of the Bible, says Pinney, have translated the word as Ibis, a water bird far more familiar to the Semitic peoples, and it is "ibis" which is more likely to be the correct translation. Pinney concludes with the observation, no doubt colored by all the favorable aspects of the swan, "There is little reason to make the swan an unclean animal."

Because of the swan's sacred aspect, however, in some cultures it is so venerated that "one avoids mentioning its name." A Siberian tribe, the Buriats of

Constellation Cygnus
(The Swan)

18

the Khangin Clan, prayed to their household gods or spirits. One of these is Sen-Serel (the word Sen means swan). The Siberians hold the swan and other waterfowl as so sacred that "one may not even point a finger at them" (Holmberg).

The shaman's gesture of "pointing a finger at an animal" and its ensuing death is found also in Native American myth. An Osage creation myth contains the story of an elder brother who thrusts his index finger into his mouth and then points at a swan who falls dead before the people. From the careful description, we may guess that the swan is a Trumpeter Swan of North America;

> Quickly the people gathered around the
> fallen swan. Its unusual feathers excited
> their interest. Its feet and bill were black
> and became a symbol of war. Since the
> feathers were white they made White
> Swan, White Bird and White Feather per-
> sonal names of honor. From the curve of
> its neck they made their war standard.

(Burns, *Osage Indian Customs and Myths*)

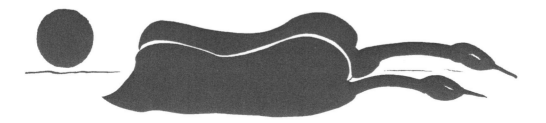

As we have seen earlier, the Osage also made the swans a symbol of the sky and a part of their peace ceremonies. Thus, like the ancient Greeks of the Mediterranean, the Osage in another time and on another continent empowered the swan as a creature both of war and of peace.

20th c. Native American cover of invitation to the "Place of the Two Swans Art Show" by Rosemary Wood, Osage

Anna Pavlova, famous for her role in the ballet "Swan Lake." Photo by Frans Van Riel

When the swan came forth

It turned into a maiden fair

The Crown leapt onto her head

the birds began to sing.

Roumanian Christmas Carol

Another aspect of the swan, the feminine aspect, appears in rather unvarying pattern worldwide. Only the details change, shaded by a particular cultural point of view. The stories are patterned on the change of swan to female human, a being captured for a time by a man. The story has been a basis for the ballet "Swan Lake" and for a Japanese Noh play. In the Japanese version the motive, according to Masaharu Anesaki, "is the noble purity of the celestial maiden and the greed of mankind."

These stories of the swan-maiden, a creature of the sky who descends to earth, are a reversal of the Greek myth of Leda the earthly female mortal and her rape by Zeus the god transformed into a swan. The recurrent pattern of the swan-maiden tale is underlain by the natural seasonal changes of the swan's molt and migration. When the swans or sky-maidens descend to earth to bathe in the waters of a pond, there is the omnipresent hunter who sees them disrobe and lay their swanskins aside, transformed into beautiful maidens. The hunter captures one of the maidens, flightless as a swan in molt, and keeps her for his wife. But, like the migratory bird, she will leave him.

How the swan-maiden regains her wings or swanskin varies. In one version from Indonesia, the maiden's tears fall on the ground where her wings have been hidden by her husband. Suddenly her tears wash the dirt aside to reveal her wings to her. In another version from the Buriats of Siberia, the swan-maiden's hidden swanskins are shown to her by her husband who believes she will never leave him. But "no sooner has she got the swan-garment on than she flies up through the smoke-hole," and "floating high above," shouts down to her incredulous husband. In this version he has reason to be incredulous because the swan maiden stays with him long enough to bear eleven sons and six daughters. From on high she calls to her husband and children, "you are earthly beings and remain on earth. I am from heaven and fly back home. Each spring and autumn when the swans fly northward and return, you must carry out certain ceremonies in my honor" (Holmberg).

As we have seen earlier, the Buriats took these injunctions for ritual seriously and prayed to their household spirit of the swan, a spirit who could disappear if not honored, going right up the smoke-hole like the swan-maiden of the tale. And we see clearly in these tales the association with seasonal migration and molt of the swan, and also, in the overarching view, the female aspect of nature which *Homo sapiens* has traditionally regarded as Mother Nature, intransigent and fateful, with a will of her own and a primal demand for worship and ritual.

But dual roles of gender, both the maternal and paternal which swans take as caregivers of the young, are important to myth as well. In Scandanavian stories the Tree of Life, the Ash Tree of the sanctuary of the gods, is supported by three outspreading roots. Beneath the tree, one root reaches into the land of giants; one root reaches into the land of mist; one root plunges into the well of Urd. A pair of swans feeds at the well, where also dwell the Norns, the three fates who ordain the destiny of mankind. From these two swans comes the race of all swans.

Because of the swan's faithfulness to its mate and its solicitous care of its young, it has been thought of by mankind, an anthropomorphic view perhaps, as a caregiver. Altruism in animals has often been honored, as in the case of dolphins who have been said to help save a drowning individual. Eros, the Greek god of love, Cupid in Roman mythology, has a swan and a dolphin as his attributes. The swan's care of the young and the female's trait of taking the newly hatched young upon her back have evoked myths among the South Americans, home of the Black-necked Swan, a swan particularly inclined to this habit.

A creation myth of the Iroquois Tribe, Native Americans of northeastern United States and southeastern Canada, associates the swan as a water being and a caregiver. In this tale, when the daughter of a chief falls ill, the chief is counseled by a wise man to dig up a tree and lay the girl beside the hole opened by the digging. While the men dig up the tree, the daughter falls through the hole, pulled in by the tree, and is dragged to an infinite place of water where two swans float. The swans support the girl in the water (very much like the dolphin) while they ask for advice from the Great Turtle, ruler of the animals, who calls the animals to him.

"The woman from the sky," says the Great Turtle, "is a good omen. Take the dirt from the roots of the tree and make an island on which the Princess may live." The swans lead the animals to the fallen tree. The soil is magical

hen two swans flew up

and between their wings

they caught the woman

who fell from the sky.

They brought her gently

down to earth

where she dropped her handful

of seeds from Sky-World.

Then it was that the first plants grew

and life on this new earth began.

"Creation" Joseph Bruchac
Stone Giants and Flying Heads:
Adventure Stories of the Iroquois
as told by Joseph Bruchac
The Crossing Press, 1979.

W ow! That girl on the

mountain

has bound in Sri Lankan style

your eyes and your soul.

How? By showing you her breasts

curved as Sinhala "O"

swanning on the mirror wall.

From *The Mirror Wall* by
Richard Murphy
Translation of Sirhala poems left
since the 5th century on a wall
in Sri Lanka

and has the power of growth (very much like the great tree of the Norse). The Princess is placed upon the island encircled by the two swans. The earth made from the island is the world supported on the back of the Great Turtle (Kear, *Man and Waterfowl*).

Rory Nugent, who made a *Search for the Pink-Headed Duck* (narrating a hunt for a species thought to be extinct) reports a myth in which, like the god Zeus, the Hindu god Brahma transforms himself into a swan to help the poor cowherd who has lost his cattle to the Great Turtle. Because this particular mortal prays religiously to Brahma, honoring the god with ritualized prayers, the god transformed into a swan saves and restores the pious human's cattle.

The authors Rumer and Jon Godden dedicate their book *Mercy, Pity, Peace and Love* to the Hindu goddess Sarasavati, consort of Brahma. Rumer Godden takes this goddess as her emblem, saying that she is not only "the goddess of pen and ink but of painting, sculpture, music, acting, dancing, all the arts. She is dressed in a tinselled sari and holds a viña, the beautiful stringed instrument like a long-necked guitar made from a gourd. Beside her is a swan, her symbol." Peter Mathiessen who like Nugent made a search, his for the elusive Snow Leopard, reports seeing natives of the Himalayas carrying a stringed instrument shaped like a swan, possibly a tribute to the goddess Sarasavati.

Again and again we find the swan venerated in ancient myth and folklore and honored by artists, ancient and modern. We have retained those myths and images and they have enhanced our appreciation of this extraordinary creature, an emblem of saints and gods, of knights and kings, a natural wonder still with us. If all of nature has instructed us since the beginnings of human awareness, then the life of the swan, in myth or in the natural world, brings those natural truths together.

The swan-maiden stories are worldwide, with the inevitable pattern of man's lust for the swan and its resultant capture. These stories, found in Europe as well as elsewhere, have a masculine parallel in the Germanic tales of the Knight of the Swan. You will hear more about this tale later on, but suffice it to

say that the Knight like the swan-maiden appears, lives for a time with humans, and then godlike disappears. The composer Wagner based the knight's role in *Lohengrin* on this story, and the opera is generally performed with mechanical swans supposedly floating mystically onstage.

A famous account tells of one Wagnerian tenor, Leo Slezak, who once "missed his cue to climb into the mechanical swan as it moved along." Slezak in an aside to the audience, was heard to say in the midst of this heavy drama, "What time does the next swan leave?" (Mercante).

In a more serious tone, aviculturists, ecologists, and conservationists — all thoughtful people — are asking the same question about the swan or about any species endangered or threatened as is the North American Trumpeter Swan. We have now seen other of the waterfowl order become extinct in our time.

We are aware now that if we do not fulfill what Robert Bly calls our compact as a species within nature, these great waterfowl and other fauna may, like the swan-maiden and the Knight of the Swan, suddenly one day leave us. Fortunately, as we will see later on, there are those who are taking action to save many species. These individuals may be great artists like photographers Teiji Saga of Japan or Skylar Hansen of the United States who have depicted the incredible beauty of the swan and moved us by their work to help save this remarkable waterfowl. Or they may be one of those who actively toil in marshlands and field, heroically engaged in the filling of a human compact with nature.

An Indian story of the Buddha encapsulates the principles of their work. For when the great Buddha "was a young man, a swan shot with an arrow fell wounded at his feet. Buddha took out the arrow and refused to surrender the swan to the hunter, saying that, 'A life belongs to him who saves it, not to him who takes it." (Evans and Dawnay)

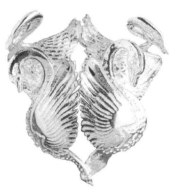

"Children of Lir"
An Irish brooch depicts the four children of celtic King Lir who are transformed into swans.

nd all the swans

Flew, clanging to Vidarbha, where

the Princess walked

And there beneath her eyes those

winged ones lighted. She saw them

sail to earth, and marked—

Sitting among her maids —their

graceful forms

Nala and Damayanti
circa 350 B.C.
from the Mahabharata, the oldest epci in Sanskrit literature. Translated by Sir William Jones

Swans, conspicuous by size and coloration, are the most easily recognized "shining marks" of all orders of birds. Even a beginning birder may identify a swan as a swan. But amazingly, as nature writer David Quammen says half-jokingly, not everyone has seen a swan "in living flesh." Even so, Quammen cites two Yale University foresters' study on animal popularity ranking the swan as one of the most popular of all animals in the American canon of thirty-three favorites. The most popular animals are, according to the study (and not surprisingly), the dog and the horse. But even though many of us have never seen a swan, particularly a wild swan, the swan still places in the ribbons by holding third place as the most favored of all animals.

Although most Americans have never seen the two wild species of swans native to this continent, the Trumpeter and the Tundra Swans, they have probably witnessed the peaceful idyll of a pair of Mute Swans floating on a pond. Thus many of us do know the "semidomesticated" Mute Swan, a swan of parks and gardens, of rivers and estates, a native of Europe and Asia introduced to America.

Once seen on all the flyways of America in great numbers from Canada to the Gulf of Mexico, the Tundra and Trumpeter are rarely glimpsed nowadays. As far back as the 1920s, the great ornithologist Arthur Cleveland Bent, author of the extensive *Life Histories of North American Birds*, wrote that he had to wait until he was nearly fifty years old to see his first wild swan. I had to go to Ireland to see my first wild swans, Bewick's, coiling in a white ribbon above the green Isle of Innisfree that the Irish poet W. B. Yeats made famous in his poem. But it was the Mute Swan in my home park who led me into my particular enthusiasm for this aristocratic bird.

Swan Lake Park in my city has long been the home of a pair of swans and other waterfowl. For many springs, a pair of Mutes mated and brought forth young to the delight of the neighborhood. Some ten years or so ago, I began stopping by the park to take photographs of the swans with their young.

My knowledge of swans at that time was so elementary that I had no idea that any other species of swan existed other than this handsome and intriguing pair of the Mute Swan species. They seemed to respond to my lens like fashion models, arching their necks in the characteristic pose of the Mute that makes it the most ornamental of birds.

I stared at my beautiful photographs for hours, and a passion for swans began developing inside my head.

One day on my way home, I happened to pass the lake and, rounding a corner in my car, I caught sight of one of the natural wonders of the world: a Mute Swan on her nest. This sight arrested me as suddenly as if I were snagged to a halt by a hidden force.

She was so incredibly near! I got out of my car and leaned over the fence to gaze at her. These birds appear to have a spatial knowledge of themselves in relation to the park fence. They seem to know park-goers cannot pass beyond that impenetrable barrier; even the wild Gadwalls who throng there in winter appear to catch on to the protection offered by open water, the lake beyond that barrier.

The Mute female was, therefore, peacefully ensconced on her giant nest,

a mound of twigs and branches shaped like a monumental throne. Nearby stood "Himself," arching his neck, raising his wings, and if I leaned too far over the fence, hissing a regal warning.

I raised my camera slowly, but these birds were accustomed to photographers (the photo clubs and news photographers made this nesting Mute a daily photo session). She, and he really, were not in the least disturbed by my click-clicking.

When my photos came back, I went over the edge into the Kingdom of the Swan. Now twice a day on my way to and from work, I would stop to behold the pair. The greatest excitement came when she extended her neck and, with a lurch, rose slowly to her feet and leaned down to turn the four giant blue-green eggs with her bill. Apparently satisfied that they were duly and evenly turned for warming, she settled slowly back down, her wings extended in a cup, brooding the eggs.

Finally after thirty-four days (luckily I was in on the incubation from the beginning), I (along with everyone else who ever came to the park) was ready for the big event. If all park naturalist Russell Studebaker's calculations were correct, the hatching would take place on a Memorial Day weekend. Rain was expected.

The city seemed deserted. The streets were as empty as if there were a televised game with the state's arch football rival. I reached the Park early, a plastic bag over my long-range lens to keep the rain off, a green slicker over me. There were at least 100 people already lined up at the fence. By now we knew each other enough (bonded by our swan-watching) to exchange smiling "hellos" and to be willing to forgo a weekend away in a countryside splashed with white dogwoods.

Someone had put up a handwritten sign on the fence, reading "Quiet Please. The swan family will appreciate your not disturbing them." The crowd was silent, all staring intently at the swans. No one seemed to notice the rain pouring down, least of all the brooding swan and her mate who stood beside the nest on guard. Occasionally, like the old stereotypes of a nervous father at the delivery room door who occupies himself with anything at hand, the male would pull at a cedar branch, break it off, and place it protectively along the side of the enormous nest which needed no more greenery.

Slowly the pen (I knew the name of a female swan by now) arose from her nest. We watched in amazement. Would she turn the eggs? Yes, she would. But there would be even more to delight us.

In unison 100 people — artists, carpenters, lawyers, nurses, cab drivers, housewives, house painters, museum directors, construction workers, computer operators, bank tellers — and I — let go a long, long Ah-h-h-h-h-h-!

One great egg pecked open by its lively occupant revealed a gray cygnet peeping out from between its mother's pale legs. Ah-h-h-h-h! we all chanted again as she turned the three remaining eggs.

We were all there at the beginning, and it seemed to us that long rainy morning and afternoon and next day — as we watched all the other three young hatch, heard her give the sharp barking sound of the mother-call, heard the male (cob) respond, watched the entire family of four cygnets, pen, and cob slide safely off into the lake — that it was the First Day of the world.

B E G I N N I N G S

In the spring, if they are free in the wild, the swan pair has left its winter home and begun the migration to their breeding grounds, flying together with others of the flock in long skeins of Vs.

Some swans, such as the Tundra of North America or the Whooper of Europe and Asia, cover great distances. Although they are in a hurry to get to the breeding ground they stop off to feed and to rest from the great demands of their journey.

*Here I glide, swanlike,
[said the Trumpeter Swan]. Earth is
bathed in wonder and beauty. Now,
slowly, the light of day comes into our
sky. A mist hangs low over the pond.
The mist rises slowly, like steam from a
kettle, while I glide swanlike, while eggs
hatch, while young swans come into
existence, I glide and glide. The light
strengthens. The air becomes warmer.
Gradually the mist disappears. I glide,
I glide swanlike. Birds sing their early
song. Frogs that have croaked in the
night stop croaking and are silent. Still
I glide, ceaselessly, like the swan.*

E.B. White
The Trumpet of the Swan

By the time they reach their traditional ground, they show inclinations to nest. Swans mate for life. For most this "pair bond" has already been made, so the problem is not finding a suitable mate, but finding a suitable place to nest. For the young, now in their fourth year or so, the pairing off has also begun.

The male swan will frequently begin the work by pulling up twigs and, plants from the lake and tossing them over his wing towards the female who is busily arranging the materials into the shape of a nest. A nest might be built on top of an abandoned muskrat lodge or sometimes a new nest is built from the ground up. Whatever the species of swan, the nest will be on or very near water.

The male might make several tries at selecting a site but the female finally chooses one acceptable place. The task might be a long one, for a Trumpeter's nest can be as much as five feet across.

Some of the wild swans accompanying the flock from winter grounds to breeding grounds may not have mates because of the death of the mate, or because the bird is, at the age of two or three, still too young to be a breeding bird. There may be also among the group paired swans who are unsuccessful breeders. All join in a group of assorted "singles" and "marrieds," and they leave the breeding grounds together on what is called a "molt migration." They may go as far as 100 miles away to spend the season while the successful couples are nesting and bringing up the young. If the swans are captive swans, those who live year-round in bird sanctuaries, zoos, waterfowl parks, or swanneries, the pair begins as winter fades to show signs of restlessness to migrate.

In early spring, I have watched a pair of captive Trumpeter Swans winding up as the days grew longer. Generally in late afternoon, they circle the lake swimming in tandem. Then, finally, like two planes on a runway gunning their engines, they pair up exactly side by side facing into the wind.

He bobs his head. She bobs her head. Gradually the head bobbing is synchronized, the bobs come precisely together without missing a beat. There appears to be total agreement.

The wind is just right, and they spread their eight-foot wings, each pair of wings clipped on the left side. They begin take-off procedures: flap, beat, flap, beat, until, even though lightly pinioned, they are strong enough to lift their bodies up and out of the water, their black leatherlike feet pushing them forward with each measured wingbeat.

Then, alas, they are down in the water again. They've had their exercise for the day, and the splendor of their attempt to go aloft is spectacular enough to halt a jogger in mid-stride who leans on the fence beside me in wonder at the spectacle.

"I wish they could get away," the jogger says. "Go where they want to go."

"I know," I say. "They're really creatures of the wild. But if they lifted off they would surely hit those power lines over there."

"I can't help wishing they could get away," the jogger says.

"They're beginning to think of having young," I say. "If they do, the young will be full-winged."

This urge to migration, spring or fall, is so strong in swans who come from wild strains that young Trumpeters (in the past) have been known to try to *walk when they couldn't fly*.

In a 1929 issue of *Nature Magazine* — dedicated with great foresight "to one of the noblest of the vanishing species of wildlife in our country — the Trumpeter Swan," Margaret Thompson Sheldon chronicled the Trumpeter determination in her article "The Trumpeter's Last Call."

This true story, a real American one, is a tragedy of a lost frontier and the decimation of many native Americans set appropriately in the Dismal Lake area of Nebraska on a ranch established at the end of the Sioux Wars in 1877 by Scouts William F. Cody and Captain Lute North.

One day, Captain North discovered a pair of nesting Trumpeters on the ranch. He was so intrigued by their beauty that each day he rowed across the little lake to feed them. The adult pair were friendly, not wary, as are the surviving Trumpeters of today.

The pair became accustomed to Captain North's visits, and when the cygnets were hatched, the young, too, learned to welcome Captain North.

During a spring roundup, however, Captain North had to be away from the ranch. The ranch-hands knew how tame the Trumpeter family was and, according to Sheldon, one cowboy had the idea of capturing the cygnets and amputating the left wings so that they would stay on the ranch, never to leave.

The ranch-hand intended to set up a business, a "swan industry" of raising captive birds for their feathers and skins and even selling their eggs to a growing market of collectors.

When Captain North returned, he discovered this plan and was so angry he fired the ranch-hand, but the harm had been done.

When fall came, and it was time to migrate, the swan parents tried to teach their young to fly, but of course with one wing heavily pinioned on each of the young this was impossible. Finally, as ice spread upon the pond, and the signals to migrate became overpowering, the adults left.

Captain North rowed out to find the young birds and take them to his ranch for safe-keeping over the winter. But the young birds, too, had disappeared. We go on now in Sheldon's words:

> Where had the young swans gone? This question deeply troubled Captain North. A circuit of the lake on horseback showed no sign, for the snow had not yet fallen. Two days later, riding over the high hills, he found the answer to his question. A scattering of young swan's feathers — a few bones — wolf tracks in the sand — told him the story.

> This spot was six miles from Dismal Lake, due south. True to their strong migratory instinct, these young birds, robbed of their wings and left alone, had set out for the Gulf Coast — afoot! Despite their slow and awkward travel, they had persevered, and, surviving the perils of one night, had trudged along bravely through the next day — when the end.

And they perished in the attempt.

If you examine closely the story by Margaret Thompson Sheldon you realize that when looked at over the passage of sixty years, it tells you more about the story of American wildlife than it does simply the loss of the Trumpeter Swan cygnets. Trumpeters of Captain North's day found the area a natural habitat as did wolves. Trumpeters in those days migrated all the way to the Gulf and nested as far south as Missouri. Later, the Trumpeters would vanish from Nebraska entirely. Only recently has there been a successful attempt by aviculturists to reintroduce the Trumpeter to its former home. And only recently have there been official reports of migrating Trumpeters once again.

M A T I N G

The ritual of courtship is so pronounced and carefully stylized that even a beginning swan watcher will immediately recognize when this powerful event is about to occur.

First, there is much excited mutual head-dipping and displaying of wings. Finally the pair comes breast to breast, facing each other with bills touching. It is then, as they touch, that the Mute pair creates a magic image: their curved necks and downward slanting bills touch to make a clearly defined heart shape. It is no wonder that medieval poet Geoffrey Chaucer associated the mating of swans with St. Valentine's day. Thus the Mute has been a symbol of romantic love for artists and poets from classical through medieval to modern times.

In the wild or in captivity, the mating of waterfowl, and particularly the large swans, is not an easy task physically. As birds evolved over millions of years to become creatures of the skies, the energy of flight took its toll. The skeleton lightened, bones fused, and parts of the bird shrank to a stream-lined minimum.

Consequently, the sex organs had to go, or at least shrink to what in mammals would be called vestigial. The sex organs are so small and self-contained that "sexing" of birds takes an expert, and frequently gender must be determined surgically if the expert must know for certain which sex a bird is.

For the waterfowl who mate on water, the male retains a minuscule penis. But even with such fortunate genital apparatus, the birds must be in the correct position for mating.

This is the reason for the formalities of courtship. The female must be in the right mood, attitude, and position (some scientists use the word "coopera-tive") and positioned so that cloaca and cloaca may meet.

The female flattens herself low in the water, and the male is near airborne as he pinions the nape of his mate's neck with his bill; his great wings spread over her while she is nearly submerged from their brief encounter.

After the mating has been accomplished the celebratory ritual — a tri-umph ceremony — ensues. The two birds generally again position themselves face to face, lifting their wings and, if they're not Mutes, calling out in triumph at their mating. Much wing-flapping and head-dipping follows, and then there is a ritual bathing.

Gradually as more matings occur — always with pre- and post-nuptial cer-emonies — the female begins to grow heavy with eggs. The nest must be fin-ished, the eggs laid. When all are laid, then, and then only, she begins to brood them. The long incubation period starts, a period varying in length with a swan species, but on average a month and a few days.

It is during the long incubation period that the swan earns its name as faithful. The male is never far away from the nest, and even if he is loafing on the edge of the bank preening his elegant feathers, he keeps a wary eye out for intruders.

Unlike many waterfowl, the swan female in her complement of white plumage is as conspicuous as her mate. A Mallard Duck whose spouse is not as faithful as the swan's virtually disappears in her natural flecked brown camouflage. However, seated on her nest, even among the reeds, the swan female is a large and easily spotted target for predators.

There are squirrels, muskrats, foxes and other small animals ready to dine on the large eggs. Other birds also can be predators; sometimes — though rarely — an eagle or hawk high-up may "stoop" on the nest, particularly if the female is away for a short interval. Then, of course, there is always that most capricious of predators: human beings, adult and child, who might just smash the eggs for sport.

Once swan eggs such as the still-threatened Trumpeter Swan's were considered a cash crop. In 1892, Trumpeter eggs sold for four dollars each. The Whooping Crane's eggs, a bird now nearly extinct, sold for a dollar less (Banko).

But swans are wary and large enough for some forceful defense to drive possible predators away. Their wings are so powerful they can break a human bone. Jane Goodall, who lives fearlessly in the African wilderness observing and writing about chimpanzees, cites an incident of the ferocity of a

And our Lord loves the old swan's nest between the Baltic and the North Sea. And when the mighty birds come soaring through the air to destroy it, even the young will stand round in a circle on the margin of the nest, and although their breasts may be struck so that their blood flows, they bear it, and strike with their wings and with the claws of their webbed feet.

Hans Christian Andersen
"The Swan's Nest"

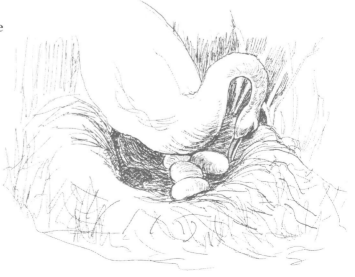

swan's defense of its nest.

As a young woman, Goodall liked to go along her English river where she saw water birds, moor hens, kingfishers, and swans. "The swans were a bit scary," she says, "especially when they had a nest or babies, because then they are sometimes aggressive. I knew one man who once had his leg broken when an angry swan, thinking he was after one of her babies, attacked him" (Goodall). Wings raised in defense of nest or young is called "display." Display and its formal stance occurs in peak moments of a bird's life — courtship, mating, threat, defense, and triumph. All swans may extend and lift their wings; fluffing their neck feathers, transformed like Zeus, they appear to grow in power and size. Different species of swans adopt different physical attitudes and postures.

The Mute, for example, arches it neck, lifts its wings over its back and points its bill downward, hissing as it makes for an intruder. The Mute male will attack, and so will the female; however, she tries to take up more of a defensive but threatening position immediately on the nest if there are eggs or young. Either gender can be aggressive. Ironically, it is the Mute Swan, who has lived

Swan Frightened by a Dog, 1745
Jean-Baptiste Oudry (French, 1686-1755)
North Carolina Museum of Art, Raleigh
Purchased with funds from the North
Carolina Art Society.

longest of any swan close to human beings, who is said to be the most aggressive of all swans. Knowledgeable aviculturists, those who have reared birds over the years, say this is not true of the Mute in particular. The truth, they say, is that aggressive behavior depends on the particular swan, not the particular species. A captive swan, such as the Trumpeter, much nearer to the wild than the Mute, may be as aggressive. One at an Ohio aviculturist's pond chased people in a rowboat away from his spouse and nest.

Other swans such as the Trumpeter will also take on any intruder defending enormous territory, as much as 100 acres, from the intrusion of any other swan. When the Trumpeter displays its wings for threat and defense, it holds the wings lower than the Mute does. Rather than arched above the back, the wings are held at right angles to the body, like wings of an airplane.

Once a male Trumpeter spotted me in a hide over 500 yards away and started to cross a pond after me. Russell whispered, "Look at him! He looks like a B-1 bomber!"

Before I knew it, both male and female Trumpeter left their cygnets in the pond and covered rocky terrain with amazing speed, their wings spread. This put me on the run. There is nothing that quickens the feet more than the whizzing of those giant wings beating near your back. "Time's winged chariot" never seemed to have such speed and power as an angry swan "hurrying near."

Once I was out of their sight (and it took binoculars and a long-range lens for me to see this) the pair congratulated one another in another display — a ritual of triumph. They faced each other, lifted their heads and called "Ko-hoh-h-h! Ko-ho-h!" as if to say, "By heavens we've done it. We've overcome."

Then they flapped their wings in a final royal flourish of mutual congratulation and turned to strut triumphantly back to the pond single file with necks outstretched, their movements synchronized, their bills pointed downward "ground-staring" as they still trumpeted out, "Ko-hoh."

If the predator succeeds in destroying the eggs, the pair will likely remate, observing all the regal formality and pageantry of courtship, mating and triumph that they displayed earlier. In what seems to be a random world, they leave nothing to chance.

Trumpeters Sequence of
T R I U M P H

Male and female breast to breast

Begin wing flapping and calling

Finishing with much calling and flourish

Victorious, leaving the field in ground staring posture

After her eggs are laid and the long incubation period ensues, the female, as aviculturists say, may "sit tight" (stay on the nest). Some species stay put more than others, but in all instances the female rarely leaves the nest. This long period puts severe stress on her, for there is little chance for feeding or for her lifelong habit of bathing. Occasionally, the male will take a turn on the nest.

With the exception of the Coscoroba, the female swan does not line the nest heavily with down (as in the case of the Eider Ducks), but there are leaves and soft grasses to pillow the eggs — eggs which are some of the largest of any flying birds.

Days go by. Rain beats down, possibly a late spring snow, but the female stays on the nest. Occasionally she rises to turn the eggs over with her bill, using it like a spatula, so that the eggs will be equally warmed.

When the need arises to artificially incubate swan eggs for some reason or other — death of the female, or drought, or any other hazard which causes her to abandon the nest — aviculturists use an ingenious machine which warms, turns and rotates the eggs in imitation of the mother bird. After the eggs are in the machine a certain number of days (for the Trumpeter, about thirty-five), you can see the little unhatched creature inside finally moving and even peeping, and then chipping away its shell with an egg tooth, a special little nail on the bill of the very young. At last, the downy bird miraculously appears.

Because the mother swan begins incubation of the eggs only after most or all have been laid, the hatching of her cygnets takes place in fairly rapid sequence. The size of her clutch may vary from one to as many as six eggs. Sometimes not all little birds survive the journey here inside their egg space capsule, but for those who do, their hatching takes place quickly. Thus cygnets are more or less the same size at hatching.

Baby swans begin life with some down. They are comparatively well-developed and their eyes are open. Swans fall into the category of "precocial" birds — that is, they come into the world and are ready to leave the nest a short time after hatching. The term for this is *nidifuguous* (from the Latin meaning nest-fleeing).

Many other just-hatched birds such as the robin are incapable of fending for themselves. They are almost naked, and their eyes are closed. These birds are termed *altricial*. If they fall from their high tree-bound nests when just hatched, altricial birds will surely die. But I have seen just-hatched cygnets tumble from their earth-bound nest with no harm done. The mother merely scoops the baby up and places it back under her wing.

Because the little swan can see and hear, it is at these earliest moments that the little bird becomes imprinted with its mother. Konrad Lorenz, who discovered and studied this characteristic in waterfowl, particularly in geese, found that waterfowl may be imprinted with anything it sees as a caregiver — even a human gloved hand or a metal feeder.

Once Russell and I visited an aviculturist whose major work had been in raising fine and exotic chickens. (Yes, chickens can be exotic, as for instance, a waterfowl breeder's favorite surrogate brooder, the Japanese Silkie, an incredibly beautiful blue-skinned chicken with silky white feathers.) This poultry breeder had decided to liven up his life by putting in a pond and raising swans. As we followed him along the edge of his new pond, we were followed in turn by a young adult Black Swan. She was so companionable that she seemed to make up a fourth in our group.

The new swan breeder gestured towards his loving swan and said, "This is Mimi. I love this beautiful little swan. She's my pet. But I would like her to stay with the rest of the flock once in a while. She wants to follow me into the house."

Russell smiled and said nothing. Later, in the car on the way home, he said, "Mr. White will never get Mimi to stay with the other Black Swans on the pond because she's imprinted with him. She will, as they say, follow him anywhere."

After the little swans have hatched and rested, within at least forty-eight hours, they will follow their mother and father to the water and the entire family will go for a swim. But this is not just a recreational outing, though obviously pleasurable: the cygnets, swimming along at once, will get their first lesson in feeding on water.

The feeding procedure has been studied and reported in detail by naturalists such as Myrfyn Owen and Janet Kear in Sir Peter Scott's *The Swans*. In short, the cygnets first catch insects (protein) and then switch to feeding on plant material their parents stir up from the bottom with feet or bills. The male is equally as solicitous as the female, and the adults always ensure a ready food supply for their young.

The young swans stay with their parents through most of their first year, learning the lessons of life from feeding to flying, from home habitat to migration routes to winter grounds where all swans become more social with their fellows and the young become part of the flock. The young will stay with their parents until they are driven away as the parents begin to "think" of nesting again.

The feather which adorns the royal bird, supports his flight. Strip him of his plumage, and you fix him to earth.

The Letters of Junius, 1771

F E A T H E R S

If you ever had time to count them all, you would discover that an adult swan, such as the Tundra, has at least 25,216 feathers. This marvelous wearing apparel serves a number of functions, and comes in many sizes, shapes, and textures, all of them useful.

Like an astronaut's spacesuit, feathers provide a light-weight covering insulating the body from cold and heat. Moreover feathers, like the skin of the astronaut's rocket, form an aerodynamic surface which makes birds suitable for flight. Birds who fly have asymmetric feathers; flightless birds have feathers which are symmetrical. Thus, the flying birds may take advantage of the lift which the asymmetry gives to their feathers.

The coloration of feathers also provides another distinct function, an important one. Coloration enables each species to recognize its own. Large birds such as the swan, whether white or black feathered, are conspicuous in their display. Once I watched a grieving male Trumpeter who had lost his mate. When a new bride was released on the Trumpeter's lonely stronghold on Swan Lake, his head shot up from beneath his wing where he had lain in a mournful position for days. He took to the water immediately, stroking with mighty pushes through the water toward the newly arrived female. Recognition was instant — one of his kind, and possibly a female at that. He greeted her with all sorts of head-dipping and lifting of wings, and she responded in kind. In no time they were swimming in tandem around the lake, a royal circuiting which passed through flotillas of unnoticed Canada Geese and Emperor Geese.

On the lake there were other waterfowl ducks of many native American species and two beloved Mandarin Ducks, oriental cousins of the American Wood Duck, the male just as gorgeously plumed and colored, the female equally grayish in her camouflage.

If you've ever wondered why the male of many species is generally so striking in his color and plumage, as in the case of a Merganser Duck, while the female may appear slightly dowdy, there is a reason. Bird behaviorists say the answer is two-fold. First, recognition of species: The male courts; the female recognizes him as one of her own and chooses from among her swains. Second, when she nests, her dowdy coloring is a distinct advantage, concealing her from the wandering eyes of predators.

Not so with swans. Both sexes in all of the world's swan species are colored the same: from the South-

American Black-necked to the Arctic breeder, the white Tundra. All swans are feathered equally — no matter the gender. But all feathers are not equal in size.

The outer feathers, the pennae (Latin for feathers), serve a valuable purpose: flight. If as few as four of these feathers are clipped, the swan is grounded. During the season of the cygnets, adult swans are flightless. They are "in molt" losing their quill feathers and tail feathers naturally; they are earth or water bound, there to protect their young.

Adult swans and geese go through only one molt a year. However, other waterfowl, such as ducks, experience more than one molt. Duck males go through a period called "eclipse plumage," a period peculiar to ducks of the Northern Hemisphere. It is during this stage that the American Merganser (*Mergus merganser americanus*) goes into a most curious transformation.

If you look up the Merganser in a field guide, you will see a picture of the male: dark green sleek head, a black back, a creamy peach colored breast. The outline of his mate, the American female Merganser, presents an entirely different profile. She is reddish-brown headed with a jagged crest extending from the back of her head, gray backed with the gray blending to a near-white.

The two birds, male and female, appear so different that they could be entirely unique species. In fact, Audubon first thought they were two separate species.

But when the male goes into molt, his dark green sleek head changes to a jagged red top-knot. His dark wings go gray with perhaps a remnant of his once natty black coloring.

If you saw the male in that eclipse plumage for the first time, and you looked him up in your field guide, you would most certainly say that you had seen a female (hen) American Merganser.

As soon as his flight feathers grow back, the male duck (drake) has a second molt, called the "prenuptial molt," and his brilliant plumage returns to its former elegance.

Water birds such as swans, geese, and ducks, "cast off" their primary feathers all at once. "Molting is controlled by the thyroid gland. It secretes the hormone thyroxin, the messenger substance that announces the beginning of molt" (Ruppell).

Ducks can fly after three weeks of molt, geese five weeks, but swans take six or seven weeks to be able to take to the air once more. Of all birds, it is chiefly the waterfowl who go through this flightless period of molt.

F L I G H T

The little cygnets grow rapidly. At about ten days they can tip-up to feed as their parents do. A swan may lower its head and upper body so that only the back half of the body shows above the water, the tail feathers pointing straight to the sky. Meanwhile, under water the long neck scrolls around so that the bill reaches far down or out along the lake bottom to find food.

The young swans are generally a different color from their parents. Most cygnets are grayish or have yellowish-brown tinges. The Mute young do not sport a knob on the bill; the Trumpeter young display a flesh-colored, mottled bill rather than the shiny black patent-leather bill of the adult with its elegant salmon colored line at the mandible.

By now, too, the cygnets have learned to preen, and like their parents, the

And for ages men had gazed upwards as he was gazing at birds in flight.

James Joyce
A Portrait of the Artist as a Young Man

41

Leonardo Da Vinci's
parachute.

young spend a great deal of time in what humans regard as primping. But it is not merely the idle elegance of an aristocrat: swans are taking oil from a gland near the tail and continually spreading it among their feathers to ensure constant waterproofing.

Too much oil, however, can be too much of a good thing — that is in the case of waterfowl trapped in the sludgy oil left by tankers cleaning their bilges or worse yet, miles-long oil spills. Many years ago, S. Dillon Ripley warned us about that.

In *A Paddling of Ducks*, Ripley chronicles his despair when he rescued waterfowl from the sea off the coast of Maine in World War II after shipwrecks left oil floating on the surface of the water: "Any sort of oil on feathers spoils the natural waterproofing of a bird and has the effect of critically reducing the body temperature. As a result, birds tend to go into the water less and less, especially in winter in the colder latitudes. Finally they die of starvation or pneumonia not from any specific poisoning."

As the days begin to shorten and summer rounds into fall, the old restlessness begins again, engendered by those haunting signals which tell the swan it is time to fly south. The flight feathers have grown back on the adult's wings, and the cygnets have now sprouted feathers capable of lifting them off. Like all adolescents they have been busy trying their wings. But the adults don't leave those splashings and plungings to chance. They begin with short training flights, short hops near the breeding grounds. And as with everything worthwhile, flight doesn't come easily.

Heavy birds like the swan must "run for some distance before they can take off. Storks, geese, swans, albatrosses cannot move their gigantic wings up and down fast enough to generate sufficient lift if they are standing still; air resistance and the inertia of the wings are too much for them" (Ruppell).

Ever since Archaeopteryx, the first bird, lifted off — or fell from a tree in simulated flight — the skeleton of the bird has lightened, the bones become pneumatic: hollow with little struts inside for support. The clavicle bones have fused into one a single bone which is called the furcula. (It is that fused bone inside the Thanksgiving turkey, the wishbone, which children save to make a wish upon.)

Certainly one of the greatest wishes of all mankind has been the wish to fly. The Greek myth of Daedalus and his son Icarus is a manifestation of that deep-seated desire, one that surfaces inside many poems of classical or modern times. James Joyce appropriated the myth for a substructure to his work, *A Portrait of the Artist as a Young Man*. Stephan Dedalus wanders along the sea near Dublin. Images of birds, the "hawklike man whose name he bore" flit through his thoughts, until he encounters a woman standing by the sea, and like the swan-maiden of worldwide myth who casts off her swan skin, she stands there before him "a seabird girl," an epiphany, the transcendent descending to earth to assume an outward guise of earthly form.

The ancient myth of Daedalus and his son Icarus is with us still. Father and son are imprisoned in a labyrinth of the father's own design. He knows it is escape proof; consequently the only way out is to fashion wings from bird feathers and to affix them with wax. As Daedalus and Icarus soar from earth, the father warns the son: "Do not fly too close to the sun, or the wax holding the feathers to your arms will melt!"

You know the rest. Icarus did not heed his father's warning, and he fell ignominiously into the sea.

The wings half spread for flight,

The breast thrust out in pride

Whether to play, or to ride

Those winds that clamour of approaching night.

William Butler Yeats

43

However, even the brownest of sparrows can fly under the hot sun, while *Homo sapiens* must tinker with engines and rockets to challenge air and ultimately space. And like the humans aboard the Challenger, the response to the dare may be a tragic plunge into the sea.

That we envy bird flight and wish to emulate the birds, there can be no doubt. We have invested victory with a female winged form — Nike, "Winged Victory of Samothrace." Our angels, both good and bad ones, flutter invisibly above us, winged creatures protecting us and leading us upward to the good, or tempting us in a downward plunge towards evil.

In the Eastern religions, Brahma rides above the world on the back of a goose/swan, in some Hindu stories he appears as a swan. The Greek god Apollo has a chariot pulled by swans. And no matter which culture or era of human beings, be it the earliest artist drawing a bird figure on the cave wall or a twentieth-century astronaut climbing aboard a rocket ship, we wish to capture the essence of flight.

That great conservator of birds and wildfowl artist Sir Peter Scott knew this. He was a champion glider pilot who said, "I want to know what buzzards get up to. I want to understand the birds anyway" (*Wildfowl and Wetlands*, May 1990).

The migratory bird's entire being is shaped toward a destiny of flight. And to accomplish flight, the bird must use enormous energy. Before they migrate, swans like other birds must eat prodigiously to acquire a reservoir of fat to sustain them for the incredible demands upon them to soar off and head to winter grounds.

Migratory birds have what behaviorists call "home ranges." This territory includes the traditional breeding and nesting grounds and the familiar migratory corridors funneling to winter grounds. There are four migratory flyways in North America: the Eastern Atlantic, the Mississippi Valley, the Central Great Plains, and the Pacific.

North American swans, Tundra and Trumpeter, natives of this continent, once were seen on all these flyways. But now it is the Tundra alone who may be seen flying to winter in great flocks on the Chesapeake Bay on the Atlantic side or in Oregon on the Pacific side.

Once the swans are full-feathered and accomplished fliers, the young birds go with their parents, flying along to learn the stop-over places, and then-at last arriving at their new homes, the winter grounds.

M I G R A T I O N

The swan family members fly together in flight formation, a long single arm of a chevron or a V, the most aerodynamic formation of all. Many scientific studies have been made about this flight characteristic; it was believed earlier that one of the strongest birds assumed the lead to break the air like a spear point. Now, scientists say that birds alternate in leading the way, the leader falling back in the echelon to rest on the wing, another taking the lead.

The fall migration seems to take a different pace from the spring one. In the spring there is the urgency to reach the breeding ground, to find a nesting site, and to claim the territory. However, the fall migration is more like a convoy of retired folk in their recreational vehicles heading south for the winter. There are more stop-overs for feeding and relaxing.

In Europe the fall 1988 migration of Bewick's Swans to England was interrupted in mid-October by hurricane-force winds on the Continent. Rather than battle the fierce winds, the Bewick's found food-rich ponds and meadows where they could make a leisurely halt to their journey. Consequently, the Bewick's Swans stopped off for some continental dining before they headed on to their now traditional winter grounds at Slimbridge Wildfowl Trust.

All the swan family needs for a winter home are available food and open water — a lake or pond which does not freeze over entirely. There are stories of hapless swans who did not leave their winter grounds in time and have been seen paddling in ever-narrowing circles to keep the water open, moving until

No sooner did the gloom of night become discernible through the gray twilight than the loud-sounding notes of hundreds of trumpeters would burst on the ear; and as I gazed over the ice-bound river, flocks after flocks would be seen coming from afar and in various directions and alighting about the middle of the stream opposite our encampment.

John James Audubon
Ornithological Biography

finally the ice relentlessly froze solid, locking them in to an inexorable death. The famous Ugly Duckling of Hans Christian Andersen almost perished this way.

But once in the air on the spring or fall migration, the swan is a high-flier — so high that many birders have never caught a glimpse of them. Joe Van Wormer, a photographer and outdoor writer as well as a devout swan watcher lives near a flyway. Yet he says, "Each spring and fall I frequently hear the faint gabble of migratory geese, and if the skies are bright, am usually able to locate the distant threadlike formations by squinting, though sometimes when the clouds are low and threatening, I can only hear them. Strangely enough, and much to my regret, I have never seen a formation of migrating swans. Of course I've seen airborne swans in formation, but not high-flying birds headed for distant points" (Van Wormer).

To see migrating swans high, high up in the vast reaches of the skies has to be the most magical experience of a lifetime. I share Van Wormer's regrets, for though I have seen wild swans circling their summer home, and I have even witnessed the sight of two Bald Eagles flying above the roof top of my house one fall day, I too have never seen that high passage of swans flying to their destination in spring or fall.

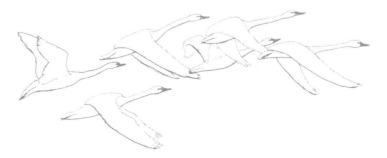

If they have passed all the rigors of the journey, escaped death through an encounter with power lines in the air, predators on the ground, and hunters unable to tell a swan from the much smaller Snow Goose, the family may arrive safely in their new home, the winter grounds.

The swan family heretofore living in isolation, existing as a nuclear family during nesting and molt, becomes much more sociable in winter. Sometimes they will live together in enormous flocks, a happy and neighborly lifestyle.

However, family ties are still strong, and even in a flock of thousands, families may be discerned by close observers. Even after a year, the young birds still appear a slightly different color from adults. Dayton O. Hyde described three Tundra fledglings who landed on his pond as "off-white" in appearance "as though they had used the wrong detergent" (Hyde).

Swans can withstand tremendous subzero cold. A flock of high-flying Whoopers was sighted by an aircraft observer flying at near stratospheric levels through a bitter cold which registered –54° Fahrenheit (–48°C). Insulated as they are, the swans will withstand what to humans is a punishing cold as long as they can alight to find a patch of open water where they can feed. Once the family has settled in with the flock on their winter ground, they may move from place to place towards more available food or they may move away from human disturbance. Too many human disturbances, and swans will merely leave.

Generally the young will keep close by the parents, and the entire family traverses a lake or pond in a splendid flotilla. As with Icarus, however, the young swans do not always heed parental warning, and they may make exploratory trips on their own. This trait has some disadvantages, but it also has some advantages for the young. As the adolescents mature and reach a breeding age, they will need territory of their own, particularly nesting and breeding grounds. Thus these exploratory random wanderings may give the young swans opportunities to learn more of an area, a breeding ground, or a wintering ground.

Each summer morning when I awake in a Lake Michigan cottage, it is my custom first to gaze out the window looking for the sea gull population, counting the new arrivals. One morning in early fall when I had already seen some Canada Geese migrating south, I looked out to see what I took to be the largest gulls I had ever seen. I ran down the steps and snatched a pair of binoculars from the mantle on my way to the beach.

Bobbing along very near the shore, were three young grayish Mute Swans — no doubt exploring the area. They stayed for fifteen minutes or so, then took

off — back to their home territory — on the Kalamazoo River. The river was at least fifteen miles away. There the parents, a pair of feral Mutes — swans gone wild — lived, nested, and brought up their young.

These wild Mutes belong to a population over a thousand strong who reside in Northern Michigan, living in a semiwild state. Their story, according to W. L. Gelston and R. D. Wood, is an astonishing tale of a species introduced by accident to a new continent. A European and Asian swan, not endemic to North America, the Mute Swan has found a niche and bred successfully in the territory once occupied by the native American Trumpeter. The Michigan flock is descended from a single pair who appeared in Traverse City, Michigan, during the record-breaking cold of the winter 1947–48. The pair was thought to have come from a flock of forty-seven swans, themselves descendants of a single pair imported originally from England and placed on a lake in Charlevoix, Michigan, some forty miles north of Traverse City.

Michigan winters are snowy, but there are many swift flowing rivers with open water, a vital necessity to the swans. The pair alighting in Traverse City that cold winter were in search of open water. They stayed on to found a swan dynasty whose offspring, in the case of a solid freeze-up, are fed by the Michigan folk. Consequently, they do not migrate on long hops to the southern states but remain all year long in Michigan, moving about like the young swans I saw who were no doubt in search of new territory.

Not all native American wild swans migrate to spend a winter in new grounds. There is a resident population of Trumpeter Swans in the Rocky Mountain area that is joined by migrant Trumpeters flying down from Canada to winter over. The winters there near the Yellowstone are hard ones with occasional spells of extreme cold, but the geothermal pools offer safety on open water. If the open water does not freeze, the wintering swans will survive most bitter cold and live to begin their migration again, if they are visitors from the north, or to move to their old nesting sites if they are resident swans.

L I F E   S P A N

Swans, compared to some other birds or mammals, live a goodly length. There is a report from the nineteenth century of swans living fifty to one hundred years (Kortright from Dresser, 1880). The famous Bewick's Swan Lancelot returned to winter grounds at Slimbridge, England, for something like twenty-three years. Some other wild Bewick's have been reported to live up to thirty years, although Dafila Scott says that the average life span is twelve years. Swans living in captivity may live longer if all goes right with health and environment.

Many dangers await the swan to cut life short. Parasites of various kinds may bring young or older birds down. In the past, commercial hunting and hunting for sport have been one of the chief causes of swan mortality. When the almost vanished Trumpeter Swan was protected from hunting by federal law, the flock increased from a count of seventy-three birds in 1935 to a count of 571 by 1952 (Wallace).

One of the present dangers to swans, who with the long reach of neck may feed from the bottom of shallow lakes and rivers, is the lead shot fired by hunters. Minnesota hunters on a long ago fall afternoon, heading home with their day's limit of ducks, probably never realized the lead shot they fired that day would lie at the bottom of the lake and kill Trumpeter Swans twenty-five years later.

When the swan ingests the lead pellet along with the food it has scooped up from the bottom of a lake, lead poisoning ensues. Without the most heroic efforts of Minnesota veterinarians, the swans brought from Hennepin Parks would surely have died. Even so most swans did die. Their death was a double tragedy, for they were part of a flock of Trumpeter Swans reintroduced to Minnesota who migrated for the first time in a century.

In England, the Mute Swan, the royal bird, has been found poisoned by lead weights fishermen use in the rivers and streams. In the 1970s, as many as three thousand Mutes died. Now the British have outlawed the lead weights, and the Mute is surviving in greater numbers.

The concept of swansong, a mighty and beautiful song sung by swans at the moment they approach death, was drawn upon in the fourth century B.C. when the Greek philosopher Plato quoted Socrates' final words. He endowed the swan with a spirit of prophecy, saying that the swan, unlike other birds, has a foreknowledge of the afterworld and "sings more joyfully at the imminence of passing on to the god [Apollo] whom it serves."

In Roman times Cicero embedded the concept of swansong even deeper in western thought by declaring that when the swan foresaw its death, it would die with a "song of rapture." And Shakespeare, always ready to take advantage of such a metaphor, used the concept of swansong, or "swanlike end," more than once in his plays.

The term "swansong" which is used in our everyday speech, is usually associated with a final and great performance, which includes everything from a baseball player playing his last game, an opera singer singing in her final opera, or a U.S. President making a last speech in office — in other words, a kind of last hurrah.

The last ornithologist who seems to have upheld the view that swans did indeed call out with musical rapture just as they were to die was Daniel Giraud Elliott. Born in 1835 when Audubon was still alive, Elliott became a devout birder as a boy before there were journals or periodicals devoted to birds. He continued this devotion into manhood and wrote *The Wildfowl of North America and The Shorebirds of North America.* Ardent birdwatchers of today "capture" the birds by sighting them through telescopes or taking pictures of them through long-range lenses, but in the 1800s it was the habit of bird fanciers to "take specimens."

Elliott's experience came when he was hunting with friends on Currituck

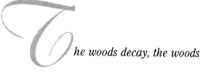

he woods decay, the woods decay and fall

The vapours weep their burden to the ground.

Man comes and tills the fields and lies beneath,

And after many a summer dies the swan.

Alfred Lord Tennyson
"Tithonius"

I can hear

the SWAN. Swan-song. All fates are

'worse than death',

Leda I offer you all except to be

human or a god!

"Cygnus Cygnus to Leda"
Richard Howard 1984
Lining Up, Atheneum 1985

Sound. "A number of swans passed over us at a considerable height. We fired at them and one splendid bird was mortally hurt. On receiving his wound the wings became fixed and he commenced at once his song which was continued until the water was reached nearly half a mile away. I am perfectly familiar with every note a swan is accustomed to utter but never before or since have I heard any like those sung by this stricken bird. Most plaintive in character and musical in tone, it sounded at times like the soft running of the notes in an octave, and as the sound was borne to us, mellowed by the distance, we stood astonished and could only exclaim, 'We have heard the song of the dying swan'"(Elliott quoted by Kastner, *A World of Watchers*).

Twentieth-century biologists and zoologists do not share Elliott's experiences on the death of swans. Janet Kear, a Briton and an authority on the waterfowl, says that swans "do not sing in the true sense and certainly not just before they die." The birds do grow "restless just before they migrate to their breeding grounds;" thus Kear suggests that "the increasing 'wing music' overhead was associated with the birds' imminent disappearance from Greece, where the Mute Swan is a migratory bird and where the concept of swansong originated" (Kear, *The Mute Swan*).

Ruth Shea, an American biologist working with the Rocky Mountain Population of Trumpeter Swans, witnessed the hopeless death of many of that precious Trumpeter population in the winter of 1988–89. In this area of the West near the Yellowstone, water rights are held by landowners, and they control the water flowing downstream to the Henry's Fork Area where some Trumpeters winter. The swans, according to Shea, were "already weakened by inadequate flow of water," and when severe cold struck, the stream froze over, cutting off the swans' food supply.

Shea refuted Plato's famous concept that swans sing most sweetly before their death, for she watched almost 100 of North America's largest waterfowl die in tragic silence. She did, however, share a sense of prophecy for all wildlife in their death when she said, "Swans do not sing as they die. But in their fading gaze lies a simple and crucial message. In our modern society, the future of wildlife depends upon human wisdom and stewardship, our willingness to share earth's resources."

Over 100 of that precious flock of Trumpeters, part of the flock which barely survived the decimation of the nineteenth-century and early twentieth-century hunting, died silently in the winter of 1989.

The Berlin *Archaeopteryx* fossil

ANCIENT BIRDS

...there were once giant swans

upon the earth and in the air, spreading their

enormous wings over the globe.

Like the biblical "giants in the earth" of the species Homo sapiens, there were once giant swans upon this earth and in the air, spreading their enormous wings over the globe. We have only their fossilized bones to tell their story. Some of these swans, however, survived into fairly recent times, long enough to determine something of them from historical accounts.

Of these ancient birds, now extinct, is the Giant Swan of Malta (*Palaeocycnus*). A specimen from the geological epoch, the Pleistocene, it was larger than any of the two largest swan species in existence today, the North American Trumpeter and the Mute Swan of Eurasia (Banko).

The largest specimens of extinct birds are said to have been found mostly on islands. Thus, not surprisingly another giant swan fossil was discovered on the other side of the world 500 miles east of New Zealand on the Chatham Islands. This great swan fossil, first classified as *Cygnus sumnerensis*, survived into the sixteenth or seventeenth century. A more complete fossil of this swan, possibly the ancestor of Australia's present-day Black Swan (*Cygnus atratus*), has been reclassified by W. R. B. Oliver as *Cygnus chathamnensis* to designate more precisely the islands where the fossil was found (Oliver, *New Zealand Birds*).

According to David Butler and Don Merton, the discovery of the bones of *Cygnus chathamnensis* on the Islands was made by accident and even a lucky misconception when E.O. Forbes, the discoverer, first heard the New Zealand Maori speak of the "Pouwa". Forbes listened to the Maori telling of a large bird which they drove into "holes at the edge of Te Whanga Lagoon and clubbed to death." He concluded the bird was the giant Moa, now extinct. The 'Middens where he expected to find [the Moa's] bones were dominated instead by a large swan," one "considerably larger than the present day Black Swan." It was only later that visitors to the islands realized that the Pouwa "was a swan and not the Moa, and that the birds were driven from not into the lagoon." (*The Black Robin*)

Another rather curious form of swan has been noted. This swan was given the name *Cygnus davidii*, Pere David's Swan. A rather strange bird, it is described as "a smallish white swan with red bill and with orange-yellow feet" (Fuller). Its more curious feature is the feathering between eye and bill, which leads some experts to suggest that this strange little creature, who showed up

56

mysteriously in nineteenth-century China and was reported later in twentieth-century England, could be an abnormally colored Bewick's Swan (*Cygnus cygnus bewickii*). There could be a possibility that this rare little swan is the Coscoroba (*Coscoroba coscoroba*) of South America, a creature aviculturist and taxonomer Jean Delacour gave its own classification, feeling that the Coscoroba belonged somewhere between a Tree Duck and a swan.

In North America, another extinct species of swan was found, according to Winston Banko, "tentatively designated *Cygnus paleoregonus*, the remains of which were discovered (near Fossil Lake, Oregon) in association with fossils of the Flamingo." (An important association as we will see with the investigation of the Presbyornis fossil, a most ancient waterfowl of the Eocene Period.)

Swans and other members of the order of Anseriformes family of anatidae, the geese and ducks, have survived to the present partly because waterfowl have a major survival advantage: though they may be flightless from wounds, sickness or molt, they are able to escape to water. Wild as they are, they may be raised in captivity swimming free on small lakes or ponds. Consequently, many waterfowl species are raised in captivity more readily than some other species of birds, a practice which has meant that some species would survive extinction. There are, as always in nature, exceptions, of course.

Certainly the waterfowl family has been domesticated for centuries. One of the oldest of the family of waterfowl bred by mankind is the Egyptian Goose (*Alopochen aegyptiacus*) a handsome fowl whose likeness occurs in ancient tomb paintings from the time of the Pharaohs.

A modern success story of breeding in captivity has been the near extinct Néné, the Hawaiian Goose (*Branta sandvicensis*), saved from extinction in its native island by an intensive breeding program at the Wildfowl Trust at Slimbridge, England, far from its homeland.

When a bird is exterminated, thousands of years of evolution and specialization and unique beauty have gone forever.

Miriam Rothschild
*Introduction to Extinct
Birds* by Erroll Fuller, 1978

From the monument of Richard II in Westminister Abbey
England, c. 1400 A.D.

The white domestic duck, a hardy survivor quacking away in the farmyards, is a descendant of the wild Mallard Duck. A fat white duck, it is considered a treat for the table, served up as Long Island Duck. The Mute Swan, the swan of parks and estates, has been domesticated in England since as far back, it is said, as the time King Richard the "lion-heart" returned from the Crusades. A bird of the nobility, the Mute was bred not for its beauty alone, but as a fowl to be feasted upon as well. As Janet Kear, an English scientist, points out, "before the turkey was imported from America in the sixteenth century, ordinary people ate goose at special meals. The upper classes were served roasted swan" (Kear, *The Mute Swan*). Thomas Yarell, who gave the Bewick's Swan its taxonomic name, passed on a recipe of lavish preparation for roasting swans which the nobles enjoyed. King Richard II and the Duke of Lancaster, hosting a great feast in 1387, had prepared for their guests not only 14 oxen and 120 sheep but 210 geese and 50 swans.

In the wild, ducks, geese and, unhappily, swans have been sought as gamebirds for centuries. This has been a mixed blessing. On the one hand, hunters thin flocks of geese, ducks, and swans. Hunters argue, not without some merit, that overpopulation, which can be a threat to the survival of a species, is lessened. This is certainly true today, when the U. S. Fish and Wildlife Service and state organizations constantly "fine tune" the hunting regulations each season through such elaborations as lengthening days or hours for hunting of game which has become more populous.

But not until the concept of "managing" waterfowl (and other wildlife) evolved, when hunting of game became controlled and laws were passed limiting the amount of game taken, and specific times were set for hunting to occur, did many birds survive whose populations would have been totally extirpated by hunting. Before the era of wildlife management, commercial hunting resulted in wholesale slaughter of birds such as the extinct Passenger Pigeon, the American Egret, or the Trumpeter Swan. The latter two were hunted for the beauty and usefulness of their feathers, with the result that these two noble species were nearly eradicated in nineteenth century America.

In addition to the survival advantage of escape to water, wild fowl have the added advantage of seasonal migrations. These mass movements up and down the flyways of the world allow them to fly northward to the fairly uninhabited colder zones of the arctic and southward to good winter forage. However, their seasonal journeys, which sometimes take them away from the hazards of freezing water, place them temporarily within the range of hunters.

Waterfowl can sometimes display what appears to humans as a remarkable ability to be wary of guns and even decoys. Recently, Canada Geese heading south became mysteriously wary as they flew into gun range. The migratory geese seemed to detect the sheen glinting on a plastic decoy, and they veered out of range safely on their migration. Desperate geese hunters resorted to taxidermists and proceeded to set out decoys of genuine (and expensive) stuffed Canadas.

Millions of other birds besides waterfowl migrate as well, some in daylight, some at night, some high up, some low above the water. Scientists continually ponder the mystery of migration, mysterious and wonderful because of the birds' canny orientation to the planet. Birds may fly thousands of miles, only to return and touch down upon the exact spot from which they left seasons ago.

Once I saw a flock of geese leaving their Canadian homeland, flying straight across a red sun. It is an image never to be forgotten— the image of waterfowl migration which is particularly vivid to anyone who looks up to see their ordered V echelon, a flying wedge against the season of spring and fall, revealing in their very passage the wonder of renewal, the hidden signals behind the order of the seasons made visible.

Northward the birds of our zone fly in spring to their nesting places, some as far as the Arctic Circle, and southward they go in fall to winter over, some traveling as far as South America. Of course, there is that wonder of migratory travelers, the Arctic Tern who makes a 22,000-mile round trip, flying from Arctic to Antarctic and back.

But scientists theorize that the birds did not always migrate, as indeed there are those like the resident Trumpeter Swans of the greater Yellowstone who once migrated and now do not. Some scientists seem to think the major population of the birds once radiated to the Tropics. As populations of birds increased there, overpopulation pushed the birds northward. Even today, migratory groups of animals of our zone tend to push farther and farther north toward the comparatively undisturbed arctic tundra. The far north also offers long, long summer days to feed in daylight, to lay eggs, brood them, and finally teach the young to fly southward.

Another scientific theory holds that it was the great Ice Ages, the ebb and flow of sheets of ice advancing and then retreating which "taught" the birds to migrate. As their breeding grounds were covered over, and open water froze solid, waterfowl flew south for better forage. But imprinted with their birthplace, they did not forget their ancestral homes. Thus, they returned northward in interglacial times to good forage and to open, unpopulated territory.

Birds are territorial. (The catbird outside my window is claiming his territory right now with a song.) Even birds who live in great colonies seek out and stake a claim to individual space. The space which they claim might be much smaller than a noncolonizing nesting wild bird, such as the swan (with the exception of the Black Swan). Yet always birds claim some space. Those great colonizers and elbow-rubbers, the Penguins, are said to attack any Penguins new to the territory who unwittingly sit on their nesting site.

Because millions of birds inhabit our planet, in fact birds are thought to be one of the most widely distributed of all animals, it is almost impossible to conceive of a world without them. But over 150 million years ago there were no feathered birds. There were flying creatures, the Pterodactyl, great unfeathered reptiles who could fly. Fossils from the order to which they belonged, the Pterosaur (literally winged lizard) have been found on earth, coming from geological periods dating back millions of years before the first feathered creature lived and flew.

How reptilian scales gradually changed to feathers is a puzzle which defies easy solution. Perhaps the scales became lighter and lighter, gradually elongating. But a fossil was found in Germany in 1861, which amazed the world — a true missing link in the chain of avian evolution. It was a feathered reptile whose bones and feathers "were chronicled in fine lithographic stone." A fossil which scientists called *Archaeopteryx lithographica* was discovered in a stone quarry. The discovery, coming at a time of the publication of Darwin's *On the Origin of Species* was, as biologist Alan Feduccia says, "a cosmic act of good will." Indeed

Darwin points to the Archaeopteryx discovery as an example of "how little we as yet know of the former inhabitants of the world."

For the delicate feathers of Archaeopteryx to be impressed in stone over 135 million years ago in the Jurassic Era and to be discovered in the nineteenth century required a set of extremely favorable circumstances. Archaeopteryx's death had to occur in a wetland area, one with fine sediment of mud which slowly stratified over the ages. The result of this gradual hardening buildup was a stone so fine and desirable that it was quarried by the Romans for paving and for homes.

With the invention of lithography, a printing process in which the image is drawn on stone, these fine stones came to be especially sought after in the nineteenth century. John James Audubon had several editions of his Birds of America executed by the lithographic process.

Because these stones were vital to the printing process, workmen at the quarry in Solnhofen, Germany, examined each stone carefully for its suitability to receive the image drawn by an artist. The first fossil impression of Archaeopteryx which workmen came across was the impression of a single feather. But this feather held a clue to flight. Shortly thereafter five fossil impressions of Archaeopteryx were discovered.

In his *Age of Birds*, Alan Feduccia compared the fossil of Archaeopteryx to the structure of modern birds, pointing out the adaptive changes. There are several changes, all leading to a lighter skeleton. Feduccia sees in Archaeopteryx "an early stage of powered flight," and he notes how the bones of modern birds have evolved through adaptation into "pneumatic" or hollow bones. The bird skeleton has lightened so much that the present-day Frigatebird's feathers "probably weigh more than the dried skeleton" (Feduccia).

The discovery of Archaeopteryx fossil was not accepted without discussion and heated dissension among nineteenth-century scientists. One of the five fossils languished in London miscategorized as a Pterosaur, the much earlier unfeathered flyer.

A 135-million-year-old fossil from China, believed to be farther up the chain of bird evolution, reveals another link in adaptation. The fossil, as yet unclassified, is believed to be, according to researcher Paul Sereno, a "tree percher." Archaeopteryx was a creature of the ground who climbed trees.

The opinions of how birds took to flying have two exponents: those who believe in the cursorial theory — that birds began by running along the ground (*cursus* means literally "run" in Latin); and those who side with the arboreal point of view (*arbor*, Latin for "tree"). The arboreal theorists hold that birds began to fly by jumping from branch to branch, then they made a kind of parachuted freefall.

There are ready examples of these two theories in action in modern birds. For the cursorial theory we may turn to the Roadrunner racing across a Texas highway. For the arborealists' side we have the passerine tree-nesting birds such as the robin or bluejay whose young seem to begin their flying by half-falling, half-fluttering from a tree.

Modern birds, from the tiny hovering hummingbird to the largest bird alive, the flightless Ostrich (whose eye is about the size of one species of hummingbird), show great varieties of adaptation. It is difficult from the fossilized evidence we have to pinpoint their exact evolvement. However, for the waterfowl, members of the order of Anseriformes , there is a possible ancestor in the *Presbyornis* fossil discovered in 1971.

The huge concentration of skeletons associated with *Presbyornis* Alan Feduccia calls a "strange evolutionary mosaic possessing characteristics of several living orders of birds." The Presbyornis, a fossil of the Eocene Epoch over thirty-eight million years ago, Feduccia believes confirms that shorebirds are the "basic ancestral stock for flamingolike birds and the Anseriformes" [swans, geese and ducks] (Feduccia, *Age of Birds*).

In 1975 Feduccia and Paul O. McGrew searched for Presbyornis fossils near the Colorado/Wyoming border "on a butte once the preserve of an enormous Eocene lake. It was the million-year-old habitat of Presbyornis....This versatile filter-feeding bird, which probably had worldwide distribution, has allowed us to completely reevaluate the relationships of shorebirds, modern ducks, and flamingos." Thus Feduccia came to the conclusion that the Presbyornis may indeed be the ancestor of our modern waterfowl, its fossil discovered near the retreat of the modern Trumpeter Swan Tri-State population.

Bewick's Swan and Flamingo

The living swans of the world are large birds although not as tall as some species. At thirty-odd pounds, they have reached a weight which some biologists assert is the optimum weight for flight. Species who become flightless through adaptation certainly grow heavier as exemplified in the heavy-weight Ostrich. The bird considered to be the largest ever to fly is a now extinct "super-vulture," a raptor whose bones were found in the LaBrea tar pits, an area near Los Angeles, California, which has proved to be a rich mine for paleontologists. The *Terratornis merriami*, a relative of the twentieth-century California Condor with a "wing-span of up to twelve feet and weighing as much as fifty pounds," may have been one of the largest birds ever to fly (Ehrlich and Ehrlich).

As birds adapted from the feathered reptilian ancestor Archaeopteryx, not only did the bones lighten, the sex organs shrink, and the "sternum become keeled for the attachment of the great flight muscles," but everything streamlined for the great demands of flight. Flight, of course, is a major advantage in a world where only a fractional percent of advantage can mean the difference in survival or extinction.

The causes of extinction in the ancient past have been numerous: violent climatic changes, earth-shaking cataclysmic events, disease. Whole species are wiped out, leaving only a fossilized chronicle, and no one knows why.

But in the recent past, as Miriam Rothschild says, mankind's "culinary interest linked to financial gain has been a major cause of extinction. In the present times, it is the destruction of their habitat which threatens the existence of many birds" (Rothschild).

Today, although birds may fly away from danger, they must alight somewhere, and that somewhere waterfowl must find is a wetland. As marshes and ponds disappear, waterfowl, hardy survivors though they may be, are threatened.

That some waterfowl species have survived to this day has been due to the hard work and dedication of such greats as Jean Delacour, Peter Scott, S. Dillon Ripley, Ruth Shea, and Laurence Gillette, all proponents of conservation.

Sport hunters and birdwatchers alike are beginning to recognize that if we wish to continue to have a "veil of birds around the earth" we must change our minds drastically toward the way we live and decide to act in new ways toward a future twenty-first century.

F L I G H T

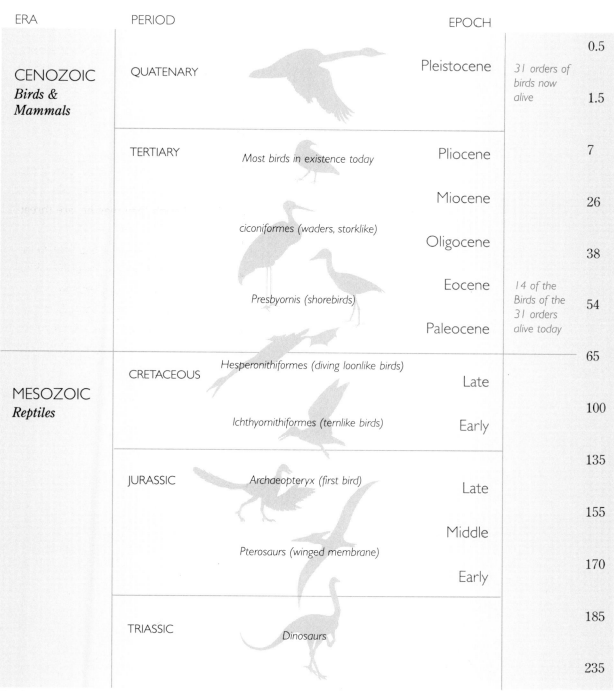

ERA	PERIOD		EPOCH		

CENOZOIC
Birds & Mammals

QUATENARY — Pleistocene

31 orders of birds now alive

0.5

1.5

TERTIARY

Most birds in existence today — Pliocene — 7

Miocene — 26

ciconiformes (waders, storklike) — Oligocene — 38

Eocene — 54

Presbyornis (shorebirds) — Paleocene

14 of the Birds of the 31 orders alive today

65

MESOZOIC
Reptiles

CRETACEOUS

Hesperonithiformes (diving loonlike birds) — Late

Ichthyornithiformes (ternlike birds) — Early — 100

135

JURASSIC

Archaeopteryx (first bird) — Late — 155

Middle

Pterosaurs (winged membrane) — Early — 170

TRIASSIC

Dinosaurs — 185

235

Note: Periods and outlines are not drawn to scale.

▲

Geologic time
in millions of years.

Naming the Swans

...taxonomies represent the height of human

creativity and embody our most fundamental ideas

about the causes of natural order.

Ever since Adam "gave names to all cattle and to the fowl of the air, and to every beast of the field," people have been naming and attempting to classify the sprawling mass of living organisms on the earth.

The ancient Assyrians, not content with mere names, began to group living creatures by their habitats. Later, the Greek philosopher Aristotle put a finer point on things by actually dissecting animals and, through a more extensive knowledge of their inner workings, came up with 170 kinds of animals. Through time, these early efforts grew more and more precise. Scientists today say there are more than 8,600 species of birds alone. In all, 1.4 million species of animals have been identified with names. Still that is only a small fraction of the multitudes of species scientists believe exist.

In the eighteenth century a Swedish botanist, Carl Von Linné (1707–1778), whose name has been passed down to us appropriately in the Latin form of Carolus Linnaeus, was so impassioned with the act of classifying plants that he set up an ingenious system using Latin names which is the foundation for the methods modern scientists employ in describing and classifying the biotic world.

It was Linnaeus who systematized the divisions of the natural world into the kingdoms of animal, vegetable, and mineral. Furthermore, it was he who set the principles of scientific vocabulary for defining genera and species, thus making it easier for new discoveries of plants and animals to be placed into categories based on their descriptions and similarities by using Latin and sometimes "less Greek" (Hogben).

Consequently, with total faith in the Linnean system, those of us who are not scientists by education or profession generally assume the world of science to be a neat orderly laboratory in which everything has its place and is properly named, categorized, and labeled with precision. Nothing in this pure white room of science has anything messy or out of place. There is very little questioning, no rummaging around through unsure or haphazard names and ideas in the way my own field, the arts, conditions me to approach the world and everything in it.

With science, I have felt safe that a living thing looked at through the scientific lens would be deftly named and everything from amoeba to zebra safely filed away in its proper slot. Consequently, waterfowl — ducks, geese, and my own particular favorites, the swans — could be easily listed and properly labeled after all these centuries of scientific birdwatching. From the time of that early classifier Carolus Linnaeus who started or at least ordered up a great deal of this, until the present, scientists have been amassing great knowledge and stretching Linnaeus' system to fit.

It will be an easy task for me, a matter of investigation to hunt out the species of swans of the world, I thought. After some initial investigating I realized that the Latin name for a single species was not always the same and that there were at least three different Latin names within a taxonomy. Now the purpose of Latin names is to eliminate confusion. A Frenchman may use the generic name "cygne" and the German "schwan," but no matter who is talking, a Frenchman or German would always use the same Latin name. Right? Wrong.

I turned to Jean Delacour, a twentieth-century waterfowl expert and taxonomist celebrated for his classifying of waterfowl. Opening his beautiful book, *Waterfowl of the World*, I felt comfortably assured of a neat taxonomy, but the words in his introduction began to warn me. Delacour feels that the common "names of waterfowl — swans, scoters, eiders, mergansers — delimit natural groups more accurately than the generic names currently used by taxonomists." Furthermore, Delacour warns of the "hair-splitters," those who want to classify every slight difference in structure and form into a separate species. If they continue this, he says, "nearly every species will deserve a genus of its own."

I realized by then there were no neat labels to be found in "taxonomic nomenclature" — the word taxonomy means the science of classifying living things as Linnaeus did. But classification is not fixed, it is as fluid and changeable as nature itself. For example, no name attached to a swan species is necessarily permanent. I found that out when in conversation with a scientist. Using the common name of Whistling Swan when speaking to a biologist friend, I was told with a certain tone that the "whistling" swan was no longer called by that name. The American Ornithologists' Union's committee on taxonomy and nomenclature had made the change. The new name is Tundra

Swan.

Whistling or Tundra, a swan is still a swan, just as, in the words of Gertrude Stein, "Rose is a rose is a rose." Or so I thought. As it turns out, a rose may be a rose, but there are arguments about certain swans. Delacour, for example, does not consider the Coscoroba, a South American he calls the "curious" Coscoroba, a true swan. Nature still holds sway, and there are blurrings at the margins in scientific discussions on classifications. This constant questioning makes the naturalist's world forever exciting. Scratch a naturalist and you find an artist. Scratch an artist and you frequently find a naturalist. (Sir Peter Scott is a good example.) The study of the living world is still half science, half art.

After all my many investigations into classifying swans, I discovered that I was more or less on my own, or at least I had options to follow. I could choose to go with the "hair-splitters" as Delacour calls them, by reducing each classification until each would be put in a subspecies of its own. But I decided to take a more spacious way and simply list the common names. My list fell into place like this:

North American:
Trumpeter Swan, Tundra Swan (Mute Swan introduced)

Eurasian:
Mute Swan, Whooper Swan, Bewick's Swan, Jankowski's Swan

Australian:
Black Swan

South American:
Black-necked Swan, Coscoroba (Swan)

Like the ancient Assyrians I had grouped the swans by habitat. I had found it necessary to use an ordering principle, a kind of classifying system. Furthermore, there is another way in which I may recall the swans by name. Not all swans are pure white, but there are those who are:

All white feathered swans:
Trumpeter, Tundra, Mute, Whooper, Bewick's, Jankowski's

Partially black feathered:
Black-necked, Black Swan, Coscoroba

Though scientists may question and doubt some classifications, I am convinced there is still an absolute necessity to use some method or other. Linnaeus, though he knew that his classifications were sometimes artificial, has indeed done the world a favor. A Canadian naturalist, Francis Kortright, gives the nonscientist the greatest help of all. Kortright explains the reasons behind scientific categories by illustrating the principles behind the terms genus, species, and subspecies:

> If you tell your friend that you have a dog,
> you tell him the GENUS of your pet. Your
> friend will ask you what kind of dog,
> because you haven't given him enough
> information. You tell your friend the
> SPECIES when you tell him that you have
> a "setter," but you still haven't given him
> enough to go on because there are several varieties or subspecies of setters; therefore you need to tell your friend that you
> have an "English setter," (the SUB-
> SPECIES) and you have given him
> enough information to go on, or at least
> to know what kind of dog you have.

Some authorities use only two Latin names for the northern swans such as the Trumpeter. This American swan may be classified as *Cygnus buccinator*. The scientist who does so is giving you the genus (Cygnus) and the species descriptive name (buccinator). However, because there is some disagreement about the four northern swans, a third Latin name is used. Thus, you may encounter the Trumpeter in field guides as *Cygnus cygnus buccinator*, a trinomial (three-word) classification rather than a binomial (two-word).

The Whooper Swan wins the grand prize for its Latin names. It was Linnaeus himself who first called the Whooper by its scientific name, thus making it the prototype for all swans. In 1753, Linnaeus designated the swan *Cygnus cygnus*, and now its name is given as *Cygnus cygnus cygnus*. Thus, while "a rose is a rose is a rose," the Whooper is a swan (genus) is a swan (species) is a swan (subspecies).

SOUTHERN HEMISPHERE SWANS

South America
Coscoroba (*Coscoroba coscoroba*)
Black-Necked (*Cygnus melanocoryphus*)

Australia and New Zealand (Introduced)
Black (*Cygnus atratus*)

A NICHE FOR THE COSCOROBA: SWAN OR DUCK?

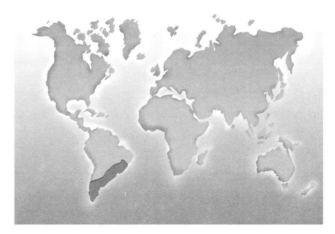

According to poet Wallace Stevens, there are "Thirteen Ways of Looking at a Blackbird." And there are, if not thirteen, at least three different ways of looking at a (*Coscoroba coscoroba*) Coscoroba Swan. It could be a swan, it could be a duck, or it could be an intermediate form of life between duck and swan. That's why naming the swans of the world by putting them in their proper taxonomic niches presents a puzzlement, and nothing is more puzzling than that little duck/swan the Latin American Coscoroba who strays into and out of its particular niche with the flamboyance of a Samba dancer.

There are scientists who might argue that there are as few as four species of the "true swan." On the other hand, there are those who might go so far as to say there are eight or even (stretching it) nine swan species. There are those who wish to take the purist's stance and go along with the "lumpers" who will lump the Arctic swans —Whooper, Bewick's, Jankowski's, Tundra, and Trumpeter — together as one species. In other words, they will take Linnaeus's word for it when he classified the Whooper as *Cygnus cygnus*, the quintessential swan, and regard all the other four northern straight-billed swans as mere variations on a biological theme.

Of course, they will have to admit the decidedly "royal" Mute, the Black, and the Black-necked to their unique place as swans. But they will have to "hair-split" a bit by denying the Coscoroba admittance to swandom and shunting it off to the class of Whistling ducks (dendrocygna) or give it a genus of its own, distinct from swans as Delacour has. There is a reason for this lack of precision: the Coscoroba is indeed, as swans go, bizarre. Even the form of its name is unusual to taxonomy. For, rather than its genus and species description taking a Latin form, it bears a Tupi Indian word repeated twice and meaning a "swanlike diving bird." The "curious" Coscoroba, Jean Delacour calls it, "an intermediate between the tribe anserini (swans and geese) and the dendrocygnini tribe" [Whistling ducks] (Delacour, *Waterfowl of the World*).

First of all, the Coscoroba (*Coscoroba coscoroba*), a South American bird, is the smallest of all those considered swans.

Weighing in at an average of nine pounds, the Coscoroba would certainly look more like a duck if you stood its thirty-five inches up next to that world-class swan, the North American Trumpeter, who can tip the scales at three times as much as the Coscoroba and stand up to almost twice the Coscoroba's size at sixty inches.

Futhermore, there are other marked physical differences between the Coscoroba and the other swans. The pinkish-orange bill—with a white nail on its end—through which the bird whistles the sound of its own name, "cos-cor-o-ba," is constructed more like a Whistling Duck's than a swan's, suggesting to some the possibility that the "Coscoroba does not graze on land as extensively as the swans" (Soothill and Whitehead).

One physical peculiarity exists, however, that definitely sets the Coscoroba

apart from other swans. Between the bill and the eye, the space called the lores, there are pure white feathers — no masking from the bill to the eye as in all other swans. This, of course, enhances the ducklike appearance. Also, unlike the downy young of other swans, the Coscoroba young are "very different from cygnets [and they] have bold dark gray markings which resemble the Dendrocygna" [Dendrocygna is a genus classification for "tree-duck" and means not "duck" but "Tree-swan."] (Delacour, *Waterfowl of the World*).

Artist/ornithologist Sir Peter Scott agrees about the dubious nature of the Coscoroba when he depicts the birds as one of the swans of the world in his *Coloured Key to Wildfowl of the World*. "This species," Scott says, "may more properly belong to the Tribe *Dendrocygnini*."

Yet appearance is not always the only guide for determining classification. Behavior may come into play. Small though they may be, and distinct from other swans, the "curious Coscoroba," when observed next to geese and ducks, behaves in a very swanlike manner. That is certainly the reason ornithologists like Sir Peter Scott do not exclude it entirely from the realm of swandom.

Once, while visiting a bird sanctuary in a North American state, I was pre-occupied with observing the many waterfowl residents in a setting that any self-respecting wild duck, goose, or swan would find a paradise.

On one shore of the green lake, afloat with delicious duckweed, a pair of Tundra Swans lazed on the grass with their fledgeling brood. All full-winged, the family headed for the water, and the adults began the morning's lesson of demonstrating take-off procedures. All swans except the little Coscoroba need a long watery runway to get airborne. So the adult Tundras were taking their time to paddle into position.

After a moment they found the wind was right, and the adult pair began to lift off. The young, even with great flapping of wings and loud cries, never seemed to get farther up than that flat-footed position high enough out of the water to use the surface as a medium to push against. Finally, one, then two of the young, to their apparent surprise, were aloft for several moments and back down into the water with all kinds of wing flapping and splashings, like so many teenagers at a swimming party.

In front of me, I could observe an assortment of Pintail Ducks, Mallards, and Canada Geese dabbling and tipping-up in a competitive search for food in the extravagant abundance of the lake.

My attention was drawn to what I thought at first was a pair of white

eing born in a

duck yard does not matter, if only you

are hatched from a swan's egg.

Hans Christian Andersen
"The Ugly Duckling"

domestic ducks in the semiwild setting. Now long friendships with naturalists have taught me that this plump white fowl, the domestic duck, descendent of the wild Mallard and a consequence of its highly sexed drive to procreate, is the bane of those purists who wish to maintain and propagate a collection of wild ducks as genetically pure as possible.

It was certainly a mystery why these two were here in this carefully managed waterfowl sanctuary. I puzzled over this as I watched the pair among the wheeling, paddling blacks, grays, and browns of geese and ducks. The two were easy to track, not only because of their white feathers and red bill but because of their behavior.

Theirs was a lordly behavior, an attitude and claim for space that I had come to associate with the aristocratic behavior of swans. The Canada Geese, larger than the two, flailed the water to escape their rushing attacks when together the pair curled their necks, red bills down to snap and chase.

One of the pair I took to be the male, wings arched over his back, revealing the black-tipped primary feathers as he assumed in miniature that same elegant wing-arched shape that I associated with the Mute Swan.

This regal pair, I finally realized, were definitely not "dump-ducks" that someone had surrepticiously dropped off in darkest night into this edenic, carefully managed setting, leaving them to sink or swim with the wild waterfowl. No, they were swans!

But when the two whistled four musical notes in descending order, "Cooscoo-ro-baaa," I knew I had solved the mystery of their imperial behavior.

First impressions are lasting; therefore, despite the case for the Coscoroba's place among the whistling ducks, I'll go with what I witnessed of their swan-ness and opt (as some others do) for the *Coscoroba coscoroba* as the smallest of all the world's swans.

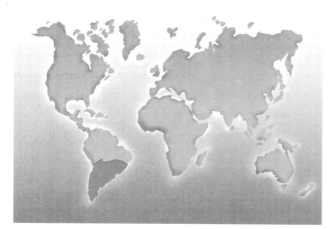

Like the Coscoroba, the Black-necked Swan is a South American, but that is where the resemblance ends. Truly spectacular in appearance, the species *Cygnus melanocoryphus* is classified as a true swan.

Hunted by South Americans for its skin and feathers, the Black-necked has been endangered for its beauty much as the North American Trumpeter Swan, also hunted and trapped commercially. In the 1950s it was reported that in an Argentine warehouse were "hundreds of thousands of skins of the Black-necked Swan to be used solely for powder-puffs" (G. Wallace). The black neck and head feathers, a white chin, and a white feathered body make the Black-necked a creature of wonder. Not only are the feathers decisive in their marking, but the red knob above the bluish-gray bill (the only other knobbed swan is the Mute) takes the magnificent Black-necked far out of the ordinary — if any swan could ever be said to be within the ordinary.

We saw also a pair of the beautiful black-necked swans.

[Near Chronos Archipelago, January 1, 1835]

Charles Darwin
Voyage of the Beagle

To top off all this exotica, the Black-necked has a little white dart on its black head which extends from bill to eye and then slightly behind the eye, a marking very like a white zigzag lightning flash in a comic book. This swan is truly an arresting sight.

The first historical witness we have is that of Sir John Narborough who in 1670 sailed into the Strait of Magellan and first saw the swan with western eyes. As early as 1846 this species was introduced to Europe as an ornamental swan like the familiar Mute which is said to be more closely related to the Black-necked than any of the other northern Arctic swans with whom the Mute partially shares a northern habitat.

The only swan species with neck one color and body feathers of another color, these swans have achieved a popularity among swan breeders in Europe and North America. They may be found afloat on ponds in private collections of movie stars, in luxury hotel ponds and public zoos.

The Black-necked is a swan of inland South America, whereas the Coscoroba takes to the coast. It may be called — if you eliminate the Coscoroba from the running — the smallest of the "true swans" weighing an average of ten pounds and standing thirty-nine inches.

Most aquatic of all the swans, the Black-necked spends most of its time on the water. Because of this trait, the Black-necked is often remarked upon as the clumsiest of the swans on land when it plods along on pinkish legs and feet, making a rare visit to shore. The Black-necked is apparently so devoted to water that the nests a breeding pair build are usually of floating vegetation.

The female (pen) is characterized by breeders as a swan who "sits tight" through the period she is incubating eggs. She is said never to leave the nest. Julianna Layfield, birdkeeper at Riverbanks Zoo in Columbia, South Carolina, awards the Black-necked the prize as the "tightest sitter," sometimes tragically so, pointing out "recorded cases of females starving to death on the nest" (Layfield).

"Gentle and sociable when it comes to other species of waterfowl," the Black-necked may be highly protective of its nest. The male (cob), the primary aggressor as with other swans, will attack, frequently making zigzag turns around the lake or pond and darting toward an intruder (Hayes).

Once the cygnets are hatched, the aquatic life of the swan leads it to the most endearing of habits: It carries its young on its back between its wings, a practice shared with the Mute. Even more frequently than the Mute, however, the Black-necked young may be discovered nestled on the mother's back.

North American aviculturists who have a good deal of experience in raising this highly-prized swan find it a hardy creature, able to withstand low sub-zero temperatures as long as it has open water.

Although a hardy species when it comes to cold weather, the swan is difficult to rear in North America. The reason for this, aviculturists say, is that there is a problem with the timing of the swan's mating. Like a jet-lagged traveler who can't get his bearings and who is still functioning on the time back home, the swans, endemic to the area below the equator where their summer coincides with North American winter, "may breed in North America as early as January or February." According to Leland B. Hayes, "Some or all of the eggs of the first clutch may freeze." Hayes warns of the necessary precautions of covering the eggs with wood shavings for insulation. Black-necked swans, unlike Northern swans who nest in cold lands, do not cover their eggs when they leave the nest, breeders say.

But extreme cold weather for the eggs is not the only problem encountered by North American aviculturists. California swan breeder Sally McConnell finds the Black-necked cygnets are "smaller and more delicate and they have a considerably lighter coat of down than do the more hardy young of the Mutes and Blacks. They need the warmth of their parents to prevent their becoming thoroughly chilled by the cold water" (Sally, Mrs. Ken, McConnell quoted by

Stromberg).

In the South American wild, these swans move in a familiar "baseless" triangular pattern from their summer (our winter) breeding grounds as far south as Tierra del Fuego and northward to the center of the South American continent, their wings catching the wind, as the South Americans say, with a "ruido extraordinario," an extraordinary humming sound of wings one can hear as the swans pass overhead and disappear in their flight pattern, moving not because of ice, but because of drought. (There is also a Falklands Island population which does not migrate.)

The first time I saw these elegant swans, although I had known they would be there, I could not believe my eyes. It was, no doubt, the same kind of disbelief experienced by early Europeans who first came upon them in South America. As I turned off a country road in Michigan to visit the Wildfowl Trust established by Biologist Roswell Van Deusen, I saw them. I had gone to the Wildfowl Trust to meet Van Deusen who is known for his particular breeding specialty, the Royal Mute, and for his work toward the reintroduction of the North American Trumpeter Swan to Michigan.

As I passed the sign for the Wildfowl Trust, I came upon his two Black-necked swans in a little pond overlooked by the neat Van Deusen house and outbuildings. I was struck immediately with the twinned movement of the breeding pair. Every action of one stretching the neck and calling out in a high-pitched trilling call was mirrored by its mate.

Whenever I have witnessed Black-necked Swans again I have responded at once to the apparent harmony of their gestures, twinned, then quadrupled in their watery reflections, "floating double, swans and shadows" in a still pond.

floating double, swan and shadow.

William Wordsworth
"Yarrow Unvisited"

80

An Australian native, successfully introduced to New Zealand, the Black Swan is the third swan who lives below the equator. All other swans, excepting the Coscoroba and the Black-necked, are northern swans and entirely white feathered. The swan's Latin name *Cygnus atratus* means literally a "swan attired in black."

The Black Swan in the flesh is the creature springing from the imagination of the playwright Juvenal when he satirized the women of Rome by saying that "a virtuous woman is as rare a bird on earth as a black swan." With usage, however, the Latin term *rara avis* took on an extended meaning. It became a way to say a person is exceptional, a paragon, and the term was applied equally to a man. Without putting virtue or chastity in doubt, one could merely call someone a "rare bird," meaning he or she is unusual.

That a swan could possess black feathers continued to be a fantasy

A rare bird on earth,

comparable to the black swan.

(Rara avis in terris nigroque

simillima cycno)

Juvenal
Satires, 50–30 B.C.

belonging to the landscape of dreams rather than to the actual landscape where Europeans saw white-feathered swans, their native birds, swimming in ponds or flying in the skies. But in the castles of the aristocrat, these white creatures could be found plucked of their feathers and roasting on spits. In the "Carmina Burana," a collection of songs sung by wandering thirteenth-century monks and orchestrated by modern composer Carl Orff, the nightmare voice of the monk tenor takes up the lyrics with the anguish of a soul frying in hell: "Once I was beautiful when I was a swan/Miserable wretch that I am/Now I am roasting on a spit, turning fiercely black."

Thinking of it as fabulous a beast as a unicorn, the cataloguers of the thirteenth century were willing to include the possibility of a black-feathered swan in their category of "rare things." Two hundred years later, the existence of a black swan still unproved, Thomas Beding asked the rhetorical question, "What Man is so mad as will say the swan is black?"

But as it always seems to happen with positive convictions, when we are convinced as the Victorians were that the absolutely smallest particle in existence is the atom and one need look no further for smaller particles, a discovery is made which turns the known world upside down. Thus it was when the Black Swan was found to be living "down under" in Australia; the bizarre sight of it was a Christmas present to the Europeans who in their wildest imaginings could see such a creature belonging only to fantasy. It became a swan no longer of nighttime dreams but of the reality of day.

On the twelfth day of Christmas, the Feast of the Epiphany in 1697, a crew of Willem de Vlamingh's Dutch ship sailing off the western Australian coast first saw two, then more Black Swans. The crew caught four and took two of them alive to Batavia. To celebrate this extraordinary epiphany, its native inhabitant, the present-day state of Western Australia later adopted the Black Swan as its armorial symbol.

The Aborigines, a people indigenous to Australia, have long made the Black Swan a part of their myth and folklore. They call the swan by several names, "Koonaworrara" for one. Other names are "Doon-doo" and "Mee-lle-bilo," all three names no doubt corresponding to the sound the natives hear when the swan calls out. Another name, "Byanmue", the bird of Byamee the Great One, the major god of Australian myth, associates the swan with the spirit of creation.

With curly black feathers, different from those of any other swan, white wing-tips, which barely show when the swan is on pond or shore but when extended in flight become a great white band of secondary and primary feathers, together with an extraordinary red bill slashed by a neat white line just above the nail and a ferocious red eye, the swan must have truly astonished the Dutch explorers. The "rare bird" was real after all.

All three swan species living below the equator have a rare quality which sets them apart from the northern races: all swans above the equator are entirely white feathered; all swans below the equator are marked with black feathers. If you ponder this problem and you seek out a biologist to ask why color differences arise, you might hear the term "speciation" to mean the process of diversity in appearance and habit of a species adapting over time to the environment. This process, a very slow series of changes, might ultimately bring about a new species or at least a subspecies.

Partially black-feathered subequatorials and totally white-feathered northerns can certainly be — to use Darwin's words about the single Finch of the Galapagos adapting to become fourteen species with specializations and markings quite varied — a "modification towards different ends." The obvious advantage of white feathers as a protective coloration in snowy lands might be a partial answer.

Sometimes, however, a scientific puzzle cannot be readily solved and then we turn to stories which will enable us to face the mysteries of nature. Myth and folklore sometimes make the incomprehensible riddles of nature soluble and express deeper truths. The Aborigines of Australia, like the Norse of Scandinavia, turned to the wild places in the heart to "solve" the enigma of the swan and of nature itself.

The Aborigines' tale of the Black Swan, with its elements of magic, greed, and transformation, could be easily compared to Hans Christian Andersen's tale of the "Wild Swans," in which the jealous stepmother Queen turns the King's sons into swans. The Australian tale, like one of the "dream songs" of Creation, tells us why the swan became black feathered:

> Once there was a magician who was
> greedy for more possessions than he had,
> and he determined to rob his neighbors to
> get more. He decided to lure his neighbors
> from their camp by using magic to trans-
> form his two brothers into white swans.
> When the neighbors saw these beautiful
> birds, they ran after them to capture them.
> The greedy magician hurried to the empty
> camp and set about gathering up every-
> thing of his neighbor's goods. He was so
> busy he forgot about his brothers, and he
> forgot to change them back from swan to
> human form.
>
> An eagle soaring above the camp saw
> these strange white birds and dived on
> them, pulling them to the ground and tear-
> ing their white feathers away. There were
> so many feathers that they rose above the
> eagle in a white storm.
> The two swans, their heads bloody, their

feathers torn away, fell down upon the ground prepared to die. A flock of crows flying over, looked down and saw the dying swans and pitied them. The crows flew about pulling some of their own black breast feathers away and dropping them through the air to cover the dying swans (Ruehrwein).

According to the myth, all swans of Australia have black feathers except for the wing tips which the eagle forgot to tear away. Their beaks are red to show the blood of their wounds. Janet Kear, in *Man and Wildfowl*, relates a similar story in a slightly different version of white swans changed to black. Kear suggests that the story might have been the Aborigines' way to explain to Europeans why their native swans are black.

Another myth, possibly earlier and from that region, involves the element of the flood, an element found throughout the world's myth and, of course, in the Biblical passages on Noah and his Ark as well. In this particular Oceanic story, a fisherman angers the mother of a water monster by catching her monster son and refusing to let him go. She retaliates against mankind in general by causing the waters to rise until the land is flooded. The people, frightened by the encroaching water, climb to a mountain top. As the waters touch their feet, they are magically transformed into Black Swans (Oceanic).

Throughout the world, there are stories of transformation of the swan to human or human to swan, "haunting all folklore," as Robert Graves says. In the world of ballet, "Swan Lake" of Tchaikovsky is based on a Germanic myth of transformation. The "swan maidens," creatures found in northern myth and worldwide, are traditionally costumed in a diaphanous white tulle. But in 1986, Lincoln Kirsten asked "Who says swans have to be white?" (*N.Y. Times*, June 8, 1986). Thereupon Kirsten, the general director of New York City ballet, shook up tradition by having four hundred yards of black tarlatine made up into costumes for the maidens. The idea of the swan maidens abandoning the white for black was Balanchine's idea. He thought, says Kirsten, "it might make us see the ballet again."

For anyone who first witnesses a Black Swan gliding on a still lake, not only the ballet but the entire world might be seen in a new way. Until I saw a Black Swan for the first time, I believed along with the classical world, and most of the modern if you think about it, that all swans are most certainly white. But on my first encounter it was as if I stepped back into my own shadow, and it moved away from me independently, a dark creature with a shadow-life of its own.

I had gone with my friend Russell to a little private lake, home of an aviculturist, where a pair of nesting Mutes dominated the quiet scene. I was there to photograph the Mutes, and Russell was in the serious act of placing four strange Mute eggs in the same nest with the brooding Mute. The eggs had been recovered from the nest of a female Mute killed by a predator. Russell's act was an act of bravery. The nesting Mute female and her male protector spread their wings at his approach in an awesome display of power, the male rushing at both of us with wings flailing, and she rising upon the nest, spreading her wings in an equally threatening display.

Even from a distance when you are photographing such a scene your attention is concentrated, focused into the tunnel of your lens. Nothing else in the world seems to matter outside that narrow visual field. Thus, when I heard a high note behind my back and felt the quick brush of wings, I was not prepared to behold the creature rushing at my back: a swan, erect neck, wings hooked in the Black's unique stance. More astonished than any explorer, I wheeled to take a picture of this ebony creature. I had indeed

been introduced, like the astonished Dutch explorers, to the "rara avis."

The Black Swan was brought from Australia to neighboring New Zealand in the 1860s and is considered an "introduced" species. However, there once was a New Zealand swan, now extinct, which scientists classify as *Cygnus sumnerensis* or *Cygnus chathamnensis* (you can take your pick). This larger swan is a possible ancestor, and therefore, the Black *Cygnus atratus* might very well be a "reintroduced" species. Like its close relative, the northern Mute, when introduced to the United States, the Black Swan found a niche in New Zealand and multiplied, establishing enormous flocks particularly on the shores of Lake Ellesmere where, according to M. F. Soper, "the colony of swans extends along the lake shore as far as the eye can see." The Black Swan has definitely found a home in New Zealand, so much so that its numbers have had to be controlled. Introduction of a species alien to an area may spread enormous havoc to the endemic population. Sometimes an introduced species will thrive to such an extent that it fills the niche of the native populations and threatens their survival.Upsetting the balance of nature and creating appalling conditions, the arrival of a new species might be tragic for local animals and even for the human species who knowingly or unknowingly introduces them.

G. S. Cansdale, when Superintendent of the London zoo, considered the "Result of Introducing Foreign Animals" in a chapter of his book *Animals and*

Cygnes Noirs à Fontainebleau (Black Swan at Fontainebleau) Piano Composition, c. 1712

Man (published in 1957). In this survey of introduced species throughout the world and since ancient times, Cansdale points to Australia, not only the home of the Black Swan, but a place where a hundred species of marsupials such as the Kangaroo are unique to the area. This sets Australia apart as a zoographic realm in itself (one of six in the entire world) which animal geographers call the "Australian Realm." We are aware today of the harm done by an introduced species, but in the nineteenth century the Australians learned by hard experience.

It is difficult to believe such harm could be done with the introduction of the apparently "harmless" rabbit, but the mild plant-eating rodent's presence would ultimately threaten the Black Swan and the Kangaroo. In 1859, twenty-four rabbits were "liberated from an estate." That simple act set in motion disastrous effects which rippled up the food chain and endangered not only the birds but marsupials as well.

In the next six years the owner of the estate killed 20,000 rabbits, but he had to admit there "were nearly as many still left." With no native carnivores to capture them, the rabbits were eating everything in sight, clearing enormous areas of shrub and stripping the bark off trees. This brought the government onto the scene and, by Cansdale's estimate, the New South Wales government spent over one million and a half British pounds trying to eliminate the hungry rabbits.

The money was not spent too wisely. "Intensive poisoning campaigns were undertaken" which did "terrible damage to the native birds and mammals." But as if poison weren't enough, the distraught humans introduced two more species to take care of the rabbit problem. Domestic cats and wild foxes were brought to Australia's shores and introduced into the fragile environment already suffering the onslaught of rabbits.

The domestic cats reverted to a wild state and left the rabbits alone, choosing instead to hunt the smaller native birds. Meanwhile, the foxes were also wise to catching the hapless natives rather than the cannier "alien" rabbits (who no doubt had been wise to the ways of foxes since the days of Aesop's fables). The foxes tackled the larger birds and killed Black Swans "in large numbers" and savaged the young of the kangaroos "when they fell from their mother's pouches."

Thus we have almost a classic scenario of compounding blunders, a near catastrophe to that contained biotic world, the island/continent of Australia. According to some scientists, this landmass had been a kind of ark after it separated millions of years ago from the geologic formation Gondwanaland, and finally, when continents and islands arranged themselves in the present geography of the globe, became Australia. Like its rare bird, it was a rare land.

The Black Swan is not only a rare bird in its color. It also displays an important behavioral trait which sets it apart from other swans of the world. Rather than nesting in isolated pairs, the Black is a colonizing bird, unique among wild swans, and at nesting time clusters into great flocks of thousands of breeding pairs.

The colonizing habits of the Black Swan long led to the conception that the bird was not a migratory bird. Its large colonies made it seem more sedentary, and it did not move with a change in seasons. Over time, however, naturalists found that the Black Swan does not move with the seasons of spring

and fall, but its movement coincides with the rainfall. If the year is very dry, the Black Swan, normally a bird of inland lakes, ponds, and rivers, clusters by the sea.

Ken Simpson and Nicolas Day (in *Birds of Australia*) point out a marked behavioral distinction in waterfowl migration. Subequatorial birds may behave quite differently from birds inhabiting the northern zones: "Waterfowl migration," according to Simpson and Day, "is very apparent in the Northern Hemisphere where vast numbers leave northern breeding areas, moving south to warmer regions along fairly defined flyways. Southern Hemisphere waterfowl do not perform regular seasonal migrations." In both Africa and Australia, large "nomadic movements occur in some species" only when there is a "wide fluctuation in the availability of water resulting from irregular rainfall patterns over large areas of these two continents."

Introduced to North America and Europe as an ornamental bird, the Black Swan has been reared successfully far from its native habitat, but has never escaped to the wild elsewhere as it has in New Zealand to form vast wild colonies of nesting birds. Perhaps this is fortunate. Not everyone thinks its introduction (or, as some surmise, its reintroduction) to New Zealand and its ultimate proliferation there is a blessing. Looking upon its great numbers as having the somewhat deleterious effect of the introduction of rabbits and cats to Australia, naturalist-conservationist Gerrald Durrell sees the Black Swan as a "pest."

In *Two in the Bush*, Durrell comments on the great population of New Zealand Black Swans which he feels is a threat to the now rare native New Zealand Brown Duck or Teal, *Anas aucklandica chlorotis*. Significantly, this rare duck did become extinct elsewhere, according to Peter Scott, "in the Chatham Islands about 1915." The significance of course is that the Chatham Islands, 500 miles from New Zealand, is also the home of the extinct great swan, *Cygnus chathamenensis*, the Black's possible ancestor, mentioned earlier.

In the 1960s, Durrell went to New Zealand with a BBC camera crew to film a nature documentary. At a New Zealand lake, he gazed out at a surface covered with Black Swans. "It was," says Durrell, "the surface of the lake which caught and held my attention, for on it floated such a vast concourse of Black

Swans that I was speechless at the numbers. Some swam singly, others in great flotillas, and periodically a group of them would take wing in leisurely fashion and fly after their reflections across the smooth surface of the water. . . . That such a vast concentration of birds found enough to eat, even on such large stretches of water, was incredible."

Later, when Durrell returns to film the swans from a power boat, the swans wheel over him and his cameraman: "Soon the blue sky above the lake was full of wheeling swans, like a great burst of black confetti, and it was frightening to watch this pageant of birds and realize that they were the outcome of the careless introduction of just a few pairs a little over a hundred years ago. As an example of how man blunders when he starts interfering with nature, it could not have been more impressive."

Durrell's feelings about the Black Swan's introduction to New Zealand carry some weight because of his dedication to preserving native species of animals throughout the world. He believes firmly in the conservation of native species. This belief is not static, for he has put it into action by establishing the "Jersey Wildlife Preservation Trust" at Trinity, Jersey, in the Channel Islands. He has set up "a sanctuary for the innumerable threatened species" for the purpose of their "eventual reintroduction to their native countries," and he has successfully bred in captivity such animals as the Pink Pigeon of Mauritius and the Golden Lion Tamarin of Brazil.

Perhaps, because the Black Swan has bred so successfully in New Zealand and apparently has not escaped to the wild in other parts of the globe, it is truly a reintroduced species. But, as wetlands disappear worldwide, the problem of introduced species has become a growing one leading to conflict among the general public who love the beauty of all swans, and among scientists as well. For example, some U. S. scientists and aviculturists who are working to restore the native Trumpeter Swan fear the encroachment of the alien Mute Swan, which has escaped to go wild and establish flourishing colonies in Michigan and on the Atlantic Seaboard. However, some of these scientists feel the carrying capacity of the area will allow for the two swans to coexist.

The Black Swan is a nearer relative to the Mute than any other swan, and they will interbreed. S. Dillon Ripley encountered a bizarre hybrid swan in

India when he visited a home in Calcutta. Ripley was there in search of the rare Pink Headed Duck (*Rhodonessa caryophyllacea*, now considered extinct), but he encountered instead a creature he no doubt would have preferred not to find:

> The Pink Headed Duck had, alas, vanished to be replaced by one of the most peculiar and ugliest birds I have ever seen, a hybrid between the Mute and the Australian Black Swan. It was speckled, or perhaps freckled all over, black with white spots, or white with black spots, it was hard to tell. It was also huge, larger than its parents, perhaps an example of hybrid vigor. The owner was very proud of this grotesque creature; he believed it was an extremely unusual, if not unique, hybrid. My impression at the time was that it was fortunate that the occurrence was so rare. (*A Paddling of Ducks*)

The Black Swan builds enormous nests of twigs and rushes, frequently lined with down. Perhaps due to its native colonizing habits that ensure a neighboring nester close by, the male swan appears to be even more attentive to the female than in other swan species. He frequently shares incubation duties with her. She in turn begins to sit tight on the nest after the first egg is laid rather than starting incubation after all the eggs are laid. This, no doubt, is another adaptation for protection from close neighbors.

This "rare bird" hatches a rare egg as well. Five to six pale green eggs may be laid, whereas all other swans (with the exception of the Mute) lay pale white or creamy eggs. Thus, even in the introduction to its life, the Black Swan is a creature of a different color.

A NORTHERN HEMISPHERE SWAN

Europe and Asia; North America
(Introduced)

Mute Swan *(Cygnus olor)*

THE MUTE SWAN: A ROYAL BIRD

Neuschwanstein Castle above Schwansee (New Swan Castle)

We throw out nothing of the past, even the dim shape of a white bird emerging from the "mists of time" with the mark of the King's ownership on its bill. The Mute Swan (*Cygnus olor*), because of its widespread residence as a semidomesticated swan, is sometimes called the "common swan," but its royalty is assured in tradition. As it floats on pond or stream, this is truly a noble bird, a silent aristocrat in the old world or the new, whose race of men revolted against the Crown but who still call the Mute "royal."

Witnessed by moderns or medieval comtemplatives as the embodiment of tranquility, the Mute Swan has consistently been admired for its beauty, looked upon by more people, written about by more poets and painted or sculpted by more artists than any other swan.

The Mute is the swan of swans, the swan of castles, estates, and public parks. Its name, like another northern swan the Whooper, is also a doubling of the Latin for swan: *Cygnus olor*, given its taxonomic classification by Gmelin in 1789. Its generic name *Cygnus* alludes to the Greek myth of Cycnus whose fate was to endure in the swan's starry constellation. Because of the word's mythic connotation, Latin poets were more inclined to use *cygnus* as the word for swan rather than the other Latin word, *olor*, the name for the species, no doubt a word used more often in everyday Roman speech and closer to the people conquered by Julius Caesar, the Celts, whose name for swan is *eala*.

One of the five swans who live in northern places of the globe, the Mute, like the four other species (adamant lumpers contend the four are really one species) is all white-feathered. But its behavior and the way it holds itself on water or on land differs from the four arctic swans. The gesture of its neck arched into an S-curve, its wing raised above its back when displaying, and the black knob above its reddish-orange bill make it different from the other northerners.

The swan is called "mute" for a reason. Unlike the other swans of the world, it does not call out. Not trumpeting or whistling in flight, it is silent. But the Mute's flight feathers make a whooshing sound. The sound made by the wings, Janet Kear suggests, is the "means by which migratory Mute of the European continent keep in touch when they are aloft," whereas other swans call out to one another as they fly [There are free-flying Mutes in England. However, the Mute is a resident swan, and it does not migrate from there.] (Kear, *The Mute Swan*).

On land or pond surfaces, the Mute has several conversational sounds in its repertoire: the barklike rasping sound of the mother-call to her young, used also in a dialogue between adults, and the hissing sound of warning which generally accompanies threat display. A close listener to swans such as the Swanherd of Abbotsbury where swans have lived, nested, and produced young in England since medieval times, says that he can distinguish as many as eight sounds made by the Mute.

Because of its ornamental beauty, particularly when it cups its wings above its back (the medieval word for this is "busking"), the Mute Swan is the swan preferred by artists and poets: the ideal of a swan. The arched neck and the round shape of the wings create a perfect hollow for the craftsman and designer, a shape wrought into objects as exquisite as a crystal bowl or as useful as a gummed tape dispenser, not to mention the ever-present clay flower bowls and jardineres shaped like the Mute.

Long associated with English kings and landholders since 1482 during the reign of Edward IV when a law was passed limiting the ownership of swans to the Monarch and to those of the landed gentry who had sufficiently valuable income and property, the image of the Mute has been assimilated into popular culture in the United States. Imagemakers of the advertising world take frequent advantage of this association by employing the imprint of the swan on labels for wine or as a trademark or logo on everything from fine clothes to vacation resorts and hotels. As an icon the mute signifies luxury, quality, and tranquil leisure. Atop the Swan Hotel in Walt Disney World are two great Mute Swans over six stories high, arching their wings into the Florida sky.

Because the Mute does not fear man,

And all the swans on the Thames will simultaneously burst out singing.

Virginia Woolf
A Room of One's Own

95

Scottish clan badge.

he Lindsays flew like fire about,

Till all the fray was done.

Old Scottish ballad

its friend and at the same time its most dangerous enemy, the species is considered a domesticated or semi-domesticated bird. If the Mute has readily obtainable food as it does in the rivers of England or the lakes and ponds of North America where it has been introduced and sometimes goes wild, its population frequently is sedentary — nonmigratory. In England, families of Mute may be seen in summertime feeding along the riverbanks while the two other English species of swan, the migratory swans Whooper and Bewick's, have left the British Isles for their Arctic nesting grounds.

The tranquility of the Mute may be deceptive. Raised in captivity as it has been in England for centuries, it may return to the wild and take up its wild habits, establishing a new colony of swans as it has in Northern Michigan or in the east of the United States around the Chesapeake Bay area and up the Atlantic seaboard. Thus, as anyone who has been around swans for some time will tell you, the Mute can never be fully domesticated as are farmyard animals. It may slip away to find the wild places again, or if it chooses, remain apparently happy in pond or park (pinioned, of course).

But the Mute, ironically the closest to mankind, may be mistakenly considered the most aggressive of all swans, particularly in defense of the young. Perhaps its enduring wildness adds to its extraordinary spell over us. Certainly its ferocious defense of the young makes it a human symbol of fierce grace and elegance coupled with strength, fidelity and aggression. Peace and war embodied in a single creature, a likely image for a family crest, a design handed down for generations once borne on a knight's shield.

The associations of noble knights and princes with swans were forged by gold and silver chains in much Scandinavian and Germanic folklore. The mysterious Knight of the Swan, whose shadowy arrival and departure in a skiff drawn ashore by swans with silver chains was seen on "the Rhone near Cologne." According to the medieval writer Vincent of Beauvais, the knight leaped ashore, "married and had many children." Then one day, the swan-drawn boat returned and, as suddenly as he had arrived, the knight departed. Like the disappearance of a migratory bird, possibly the inspiration for this medieval story, the Knight of the Swan vanished and "was seen no more." He appears, however, in Wagnerian opera, and may be witnessed embodied in his role in *Lohengrin*.

Another version of German medieval romance has a knight seizing the gold chain a swan-maiden lays aside on the bank while she is bathing. Because the knight has her magic chain, she cannot fly away. He marries her and she has seven sons, "each with a golden necklace by which they may become swans" (McCulloch, *Eddic*). In Hans Christian Andersen's tale, The *Wild Swans*, eleven brothers, all young princes, are transformed by the spell of a wicked stepmother into eleven swans with golden crowns.

Merging folklore and history, two noble families of Normandy, the de Bouillons and the de Cleves, claimed descent from the Knight of the Swan. Each family adopted the white swan as their emblem. One of the family in fact, not in fantasy, married and became a Queen when Mary Bohun (the de Bouillon name transformed by usage to Bohun) married Henry IV of England. Their heir, Henry V, Shakespeare's ideal king, carried a white swan's emblem on his battle flag when he overcame the French at the Battle of Agincourt (Kear, *Man and Wildfowl*).

Thus not only an image of tranquility in the medieval mind, the swan, particularly the Mute, is emblematic to humans of nobility. Natural aristocrats in their regal and elegant bearing, all swans have a biological behavior which leads a scientist such as Paul A. Johnsgard to say that swans act naturally "in keeping with the royalty often ascribed to them." Their behavior in nature, requiring more space for nesting, more time for incubation and bringing up the young, contrasts with their waterfowl relatives, the more economical ducks. Johnsgard maintains that the swan has a "social behavior based on a nonegalitarian doctrine of differential social status," and that in terms of reproduction, the swan's form of "conspicuous consumption" of time and space may curtail its production of young in an environment where resources are limited.

Swans are intolerant of their own species nearby when they are nesting, but they do tolerate ducks nesting close to them. It is not only their behavior

Derived from detail of ornamental design on the wall of a room in Caesar Augustus' son-in law's house.

97

in the wild requiring a luxury of time and space, while the swan's duck cousins tend in Johnsgard's words "toward a democratic society," which accounts for their royal image. There is the actual connection to the monarchy and all the pomp and circumstance accompanying the keeping of swans by king and noble as well. The ownership of swans is colored with tradition, and swan-keeping goes back historically in England at least 700 years.

The English, particularly experts on the Mute Swan species, have theorized over time as to whether or not the Mute is indeed a native bird, one endemic to the British Isles. Some suggest that the Mute species might have been an introduced species, brought to Britain in the twelfth century by King Richard Coeur de Lion (the Lionheart) when he returned from the crusades around the year 1194 A.D.

Other authorities maintain that there was a native population before Richard's time, or at least an established population of Mute Swans. N. F. Ticehurst, in his work *The Swan-Marks of Lincolnshire* (1934), argues that indeed the Mute was in England before Richard's return. But, says Ticehurst, "the origin of the birds' status as a royal fowl seems to have been lost in the mists of time."

However, Ticehurst cites a report of an established Mute population by at least 1186 in the writing of medieval historian Giraldus Cambrensis (1146–1220) as definite proof that an eastern area of England, The Fenland, was the ancient home of an indigenous race of Mute Swans. These Mutes were also first "reduced to the condition of semidomesticity," swans bred in captivity.

The Latin passage written by Giraldus, the friend of King Richard and St. Hugh, which Ticehurst points out as support to his belief that the Mute was indeed in England before King Richard's return, is an account of the installation of Hugh as Bishop of Lincoln in 1186 (Ticehurst's pivotal date). Later elevated to sainthood and known as St. Hugh of Lincoln, the Saint is traditionally pictured with his emblem, a pet swan, which Ticehurst notes should be a Whooper rather than the Mute species.

The Latin passage by Giraldus Cambrensis makes a distinction between the two species of swan. One, a wild swan who flew into the Bishop's residential park, is quite clearly a Whooper, whom the medieval historian describes as exhibiting no knob above the bill (as does the Mute). Rather than the black knob, the strange swan has instead a "becomingly yellow patch on the bill" (as does the Whooper). This strange swan (and the common Latin word for swan *olor* is used for him) overcomes the resident population of swans (here Giraldus uses the poet's word *cygnus* for the Mute) and the wild swan stays with the Bishop.

Some taxonomists say that Linnaeus, father of taxonomy, who first gave the Latin name to the Whooper, did not make a distinction between the two species. But 600 years before Linnaeus, Giraldus does make a distinction in his clear use of the word *olor* (as a wild swan, Whooper), and *cygnus* (Mute). For those who want to investigate this passage further, the translation is in the note to this chapter.

Another curious fact about the use of the word *cygnus* came to light when a classicist friend was translating the medieval Latin passage. It was she who noticed the distinction in Geraldus' use of *olor* and *cygnus*. That sent me to a Medieval Latin dictionary where I also discovered the Latin word *signo* (which is sounded like *cigno*, the medieval spelling), and is a word from which we get our word "sign." One of the meanings for *signo* in medieval Latin is "a swan marked with a sign" — or the swan-marks, the special marks on the upper bill, put there to show ownership.

All swans of England who are unmarked and free belong to the Crown. Even today, unmarked swans are the Queen's own birds, a royal prerogative since early time. This ownership is presided over by the Royal Swan-Master, an office which is held to this day. Swans have been, and are yet, considered valuable property. In the past only the Monarch and titled landholders could own a game of swans and maintain the right to place a special device on their bill to signify ownership of them.

Gradually ownership expanded to include freeholders, property owners who devised an individual mark registered on the rolls of the shire. A family swan-mark descended from father to son or through a daughter and her heirs. Thus, a code of customs grew, made legal and formalized by officials of the Crown, and swan ownership became a status symbol.

Towards the close of the fifteenth century the business of owning and

The King's Swan Mark
Used earlier than Henry VIII

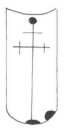

Lord de la Ware

The Abbot of Croyland

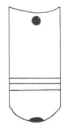

Sir Miles Bussy

breeding swans was a totally organized affair. The marking of young swans also began to take on an established ritual which had and still has all the extravagance and panoply appropriate to owning such a noble possession as a swan. The ceremony of marking the swan's bill with hatch marks was governed by strict rules and became known as "swan-hopping" or "swan-upping."

Thus the long tradition of the swan as possession of nobility and the affluent endures today. In England the swan-upping ceremony occurs annually during the third week of July when the adult swans are in molt and are therefore flightless.

The ritual has all the pomp and circumstance of a royal hunt, when costumed men, representatives of the monarch and the two ancient guilds, put out in old skiffs on the Thames River, their boats flying from the stern a red flag emblazoned with the image of the Mute and the crest of Royalty or the two ancient guilds, the Vintners and the Dyers. These two guilds still maintain the right to mark swans by royal decree.

The boatsmen, "swan-hoppers" or "swan-uppers," catch the flightless adults to renew the hatch marks of the bill which might have faded over the year. The cygnets, having never yet become air-borne, are caught and marked with newly made swan-marks. At this time the birds are all pinioned so that the Thames will be forever their home, a home near human habitation.

The Mute, although semidomesticated and nonmigratory in England, may also be a feral (wild) swan. Classified as a native Eurasian swan, the Mute may yet be found in pockets across Europe and Asia, although its range does not encompass the vast range of its fellow Eurasians, Whooper and Bewick's. An isolated group of Mutes became known as the "Polish Swan" with its own Latin name of *Cygnus immutabilis* for the subspecies. Yarrell, who gave the Polish Swan its name, called it *immutabilis* (unchanging) to designate the constant of white coloration from cygnet to adult, for the cygnets are white, not dusky gray.

The term "Royal" for the Mute is used to designate the black-legged Mute, sometimes called the "English" Mute. According to biologist and aviculturist Roswell Van Deusen, who has spent a good deal of time and energy on this subject (the breeding of Royals is his particular specialty), the term "Royal" is used to distinguish the Mute from the Polish subspecies. The Royal is "descended from the Queen's flock in England. The English Mutes are characterized by a deep orange-red bill and jet black feet. Their cygnets are dusky when hatched. The Polish Mute, in contrast, has a brighter orange bill and light buff-colored feet. Their cygnets are nearly white when hatched with a tinge of buff" (Van Deusen quoted by Stromberg, *Swan Breeding and Management*).

English stamps honoring the swans of Abbotsbury in Dorset
Reproduced courtesy of the British Post Office
David Gentleman, designer

Thus, when that consummate birdwatcher the Swan of Avon (who made reference to well over fifty species of birds in his plays), William Shakespeare wrote that "all the water in the ocean can never turn the swan's legs to white"

he had obviously observed only the Queen's own swans, the "Royal" Mute. He had never beheld the Polish Mute, its leucistic phase materializing in the white cygnets following at the pale, pale feet of their Polish mother swan, her gesture as aristocratic as any of the other swans of the world.

The poet Edmund Spenser, Shakespeare's contemporary, united the swan of England with the River Thames in one of his most elegant poems, "Prothalamion," written in honor of a double marriage of Ladies Elizabeth and Katherine Somerset, daughters of the Earl. In this allegorical poem, Spenser uses the purity of the swan and their aristocracy to link them with the River Thames and the noble ladies:

> So purely white they were,
> That even the gentle streame, the which
> them bare,
> Seem'd foule to them, and had his bil-
> lowes spare,
> To wet their fayre plumes with water not
> so fayre,
> And marre their beauties bright,
> That shone as heaven's light,
> Against their Brydale day, which was not
> long;
> Sweete Themmes! runne softy, till I end
> my song.

Translation of Giraldus Cambrensis's Latin

When the Bishop Hugh, as yet uninstalled as Bishop, was first brought to Lincolnshire to his manorhouse almost eight miles distant from the city of Lincoln near Stowe filled delightfully with forests and fens, a swan (olor) never before seen there flew in. This swan (olor) within a few days suppressed and did away the swans (cignos) many of which he the swan (olor) discovered there: nevertheless one of the feminine sex of swans (cignos) was kept by the swan (olor) for her society and not to mate with.

Indeed he (the swan olor) was altogether so much stronger than a swan (cigno), as a swan (cignos) is more powerful than a goose. Indeed in all respects, especially in color and dazzling whiteness he (olor) was very like a swan (cignus) except for the amount, even at this distance, that he did not present the swelling on his beak nor the duskiness (of it) in the manner of other swans (cignos). He had a flat place on his beak with a becomingly yellow color distinct from his head and the upper part of his neck.

Translated by Mary Linda Yeakey

THE ARCTIC SWANS

Europe and Asia
Whooper (*Cygnus cygnus cygnus*)
Bewick's (*Cygnus cygnus bewickii*)
Jankowski's (*Cygnus cygnus jankowskii*) (The
Eastern Bewick's)

North America
Tundra (*Cygnus cygnus columbianus*)
Trumpeter (*Cygnus cygnus buccinator*)

THE WHOOPER SWAN

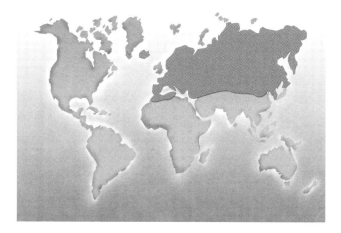

19th century Victorian representation
of Whooper Swan.

Earlier swan fanciers like the Earl of Lonsdale sometimes called the Whooper Swan by the Latin Cygnus musicus (literally "musical swan") to give tribute to the swan's musical call of whoop, whoop, whoop, or as the ancient Greeks put it, tiotiotiotiotinx. Another vernacular or common name for the Whooper is "wild swan," used throughout Europe, the French using the same term as *cygne sauvage*.

The Whooper, a large Eurasian swan weighing less than the semidomestic Mute, presents itself to knowing swan watchers as differing markedly from the Mute. An art historian might characterize the lines of the Mute as baroque and the four Northern swans, of which the Whooper is one, as neoclassical, thus contrasting the S-curve profile of Mute as opposed to the simpler classical lines of the Whooper.

All four northern swans are straight necked and white feathered, and all four have a call which varies — some with a high range, others with the low sonorous call of the Trumpeter. The Whooper, of course, holds its place in taxonomy, for as you will remember, it was first classified by Linnaeus.

Chosen by Linnaeus to give the first Latin descriptive name to the swan, the Whooper is sometimes thought of as the type or model of the Northern swans. This might have been the Linnean intent, for the Whooper's name is very special in its grammatical construction: all three Latin names are nouns. For that matter, they are the same noun: *cygnus* tripled.

As a rule when a scientist following Linnaeus's system of description gives a name to a species, the scientist first lists the genus. In the case of human beings the genus is Homo (man). An adjective to describe the genus is used for the species — in man's case the adjective is sapiens, which means literally, and with a marked anthropocentric bias, "wise," or putting a more prideful spin on it, "one who knows the truth."

In the Whooper's case, however, as has been noted, the word following the genus is another noun. To show the Whooper's close identity with the other northern swans, *cygnus* is used again as a descriptive name. The subequatorial swans do not share this confusion, or to use a more scientific word, conspecificity (which means they are alike but different).

All of the northern swans thus share similarities, and each has a three

104

word Latin name to denote this — perhaps. If you are looking at a chart of the International Wild Waterfowl Association, a society founded by the great taxonomist Jean Delacour, the three word Latin name holds true. But if you are looking through the American Ornithologists' Union's Checklist, you will find the Whooper listed merely as *Cygnus cygnus*.

The problem of the four northern swans doesn't stop there. The American Ornithologists' Union's Committee responsible for a checklist of North American birds recognizes there is a problem in classifying the Northerners. The AOU took up the problem by saying the "relationship of *Cygnus cygnus* (Whooper), *Cygnus columbianus* (Tundra), and *Cygnus buccinator* are uncertain at the species level. *Cygnus cygnus* and *Cygnus buccinator* have been considered conspecific by some authors; an extreme view unites all three into a single species [the lumpers], despite geographical overlap in the ranges of the two old World forms [Whooper and Bewick's]. For the present it seems best to retain all three as distinct species." The splitters win!

Four Arctic Swans (left to right)
Whooper, Trumpeter, Bewick's, Tundra

Now if you've had a heavy enough dose of what Audubon called "closet" naturalism, that is bookish learning and discussion, and you go out into the field — and you'll have to make a snowy circumpolar journey to the Arctic to find all four — you will see and hear the four Northerners are alike but different: in appearance, somewhat different; in their calls, decidedly different.

All are white feathered, straight billed. Customarily they hold their necks straighter than the Mute. Two are larger than the other two, but it is by their bills "ye shall know them." And that is no doubt the reason for all the discussion. In the field it is difficult to discern the difference in the species (or subspecies) of high-flying swans by looking at their bills.

However, if you get close enough your field glasses will tell you the difference, or if you listen to the calls, you can hear the difference.

The syrinx (a bird's version of the human voice box organ, the larnyx) of the two North Americans, Tundra and Trumpeter, are markedly different. Thus the physical construction of the voice box and the convolution of the trachea actually produce a different sound, the former a high pitched whistling sound, the latter a sonorous trumpeting. It is the physical difference of the syrinx and trachea which finally enabled Sir John Richardson to positively dis-

Art Nouveau swan (Whooper)
by M.P. Verneail
lithographed portfolio
L'animal dans la decoration
French, 19th century

tinguish the two American swans. Richardson was preceded by Yarrell in distinguishing the Eurasian Whooper and Bewick's swans (Banko).

Certainly the Whooper, whooping it up at near stratospheric levels, is the most far ranging in its distribution of all the swans. On its winter grounds stretching from Iceland on the west to the Bering Sea on the east it sounds out its own particular call of whoop! whoop! whoop!

When migrating to its winter habitats in Europe and Asia from its breeding ground close to the Arctic circle, the Whooper is so far flung in its range that a Briton might safely call it a "British" swan and a Japanese might just as safely call it a "Japanese" swan. But the Russian would be the most assured of all in calling the Whooper a "Russian," for the heaviest concentration of nesting Whoopers is in Russia. The Bewick's and its near-twin, the Jankowski's, are also widespread through Europe and Asia — but those two are another taxonomic problem better saved for later.

The difference in the bills which sets off the four Northern swans in appearance may be established through color patterns. The Medieval historian Giraldus Cambrensis distinguished the Whooper from the Mute by the bills and remarked on the yellow spot or color pattern of the strange swan who flew into the Bishop's residence to become his pet and a saint's emblem.

The Whooper is larger than its fellow Eurasian Bewick's and also the Tundra (North American), but all have black bills with yellow patches at the base (nearest the eye). The North American Trumpeter (slightly larger than the Whooper) has the same straight black bill, but rather than a yellow patch on the bill the Trumpeter's bill appears totally black with an elegant salmon red line along the mandible, sometimes called the "grinning" line.

In the northern European continent that it visits the Whooper can be distinguished from the Bewick's, which also winters in North Europe, primarily by its call. The Whooper releases a resonant musical "trombone-like sound" (Hillprecht) which is also described as a melodious "ang." The Bewick's, in contrast, has a call which is lyrically soft, "like silver bells" (Hillprecht) a kind of "goonk" or when excited a "goo-a lookh."

The bills of the two swans also differ. The Whooper's yellow patch is larger than the Bewick's and it reaches to the nostril. Thus, the Whooper's head appears to be more triangular or wedge shaped (certainly more so than the Mute). The Bewick's yellow marks have been found to be almost as individualized as a human thumb print (a great deal more on that later).

Noted ornithologist Arthur Cleveland Bent in his far-reaching study *Life Histories of North American Birds*, included the Whooper as an American because of its status as a breeding bird in southern Greenland. Writing in 1923, Bent finds the Whooper vanished from the Greenland area thirty years previous to his study. Bent takes note of the Whooper's residence in Greenland but believes the swan to have been exterminated there "by the natives who pursued and killed the young birds when molting and unable to fly" (Bent).

The Whooper was also hunted in Iceland where it still nests. Dr. G. Hartwig, a nineteenth-century American, in the section on "Man and Nature" in *The Polar and Tropical Worlds* (1877) carefully notes the taxonomic classification of all birds and mammals, but when writing of the Whooper over a century ago he left it to the reader's imagination to guess the species of swan described as witnessed in Iceland. However, St. Hugh's Mute was a Whooper and G. Hartwig's generic "swans" were most certainly the far-flung Whooper. A modern bird-fancier will no doubt pause at Hartwig's report of these beautiful creatures hunted "even to the solitary waste of Iceland" over a hundred years ago:

> The wild swan is frequently shot or
> caught for his feathers, which bring in
> many a dollar to the fortunate huntsman.

This noble bird frequents both salt and brackish water along the coasts and inland lakes and rivers, where it is seen either in single pairs or congregated in large flocks. To build its nest, (which is said to resemble closely the Flamingo), being a large mound composed of mud, rushes, grass and stones, with a cavity at top lined with soft down, it retires to some solitary uninhabited spot. Much has been said in ancient times of the singing of the swan and the beauty of its dying notes; but in truth, the voice of the swan is very loud, shrill and harsh, though when high in the air, and modulated by the winds the note or whoop of an assemblage of them is not unpleasant to the ear.

It has a peculiar charm in the unfrequented wastes of Iceland where it agreeably interrupts the profound silence that reigns around. (Hartwig, *The Polar and Tropical Worlds*)

The Icelandic flock, unlike the Greenland Whoopers, have survived to this day. One arm of their migration winters in Britain where artist/aviculturist Peter Scott may look upon the Whoopers from his observatory window using field glasses once belonging to Thomas Bewick, and return to his easel to render on canvas their arrowsure flight above the English countryside.

Of a painting entitled "Whooper Swans at Morning Flight" (1967), Scott remarks on the "special challenge" in painting the Whoopers "outlined against the light," the soft morning sunrays coming through their feathers, their blue shadowed forms fringed with a near celestial white (Scott, *Observations of Wildlife*).

In his book *Observations of Wildlife*, Sir Peter comments on the Whooper's migratory origins, hazarding a guess as from whence they come: "They may be

part of the 5,000 Icelandic-bred population, of which 4,500 are believed to winter in Britain and Ireland. As yet we do not know what proportion of our winter whoopers come down from Scandinavia and the U.S.S.R."

At the other extreme of the Whooper's range, the Far East, another artist, this one with a camera rather than a paint brush, is at work creating astonishingly beautiful photographs of the Whoopers awakening in the snows of northern Japan.

Reproduced in *Life* magazine, these photographs by Teiji Saga are truly a wonder, not only for their startling beauty but for the fact the Whooper, now common in Japan, was once on the verge of extinction. Today, according to *Life* reporters Sue Allison and Carol Simons, the Whooper population has "burgeoned to 33,000 strong."

It was the endangerment of the Whooper species which drew Teiji Saga into his incredible kingdom of swan photography. "If ever there was a zen of swan watching," say Allison and Simons, "Saga has mastered it. Inspired by a 1965 TV documentary about a Hokkaido farmer who championed birds, Saga, an amateur photographer, set off to meet him. There Saga found a meaning he felt his life had lacked. His winter regime today is more meditative discipline than hobby. He drives some 5,000 miles and spends about $15,000 to don long underwear, down parka and fur hat, and spend all day, every day following swans. He tows his cameras on a sled. He eats nothing — he doesn't even carry a thermos of hot tea. 'I am all alone, just looking and looking,' he says" (*Life*).

Peter Scott in England and Teiji Saga in Japan are swan hunters of a new and different breed. Their challenge of course is to capture visually the world of the swan. Each is an ardent conservator of the swan, each has followed a difficult, sometimes arduous path to seek out the prize and to maintain its existence. But of course they present profiles on the obverse of the hunting coin.

Swans are still hunted and killed today by hunters with guns who take their prizes home to have stuffed as illegal or legal trophies. Yes, legal as well. Some states in the United States still permit hunting of swans. But there are swan watchers like Scott and Saga whose aim is to seize the trophy of the swan on canvas or on film. Their magnificent images have done a great deal to heighten our awareness of these magnificent birds.

There are hunters, too, who consider the swan a non–game bird. Such a hunter is a friend of mine, Jim Thomas, a fine and skillful hunter of game birds who, after returning from a hunting trip to Wyoming, told me that he saw "three Trumpeters flying in a line against a late fall sky. That encounter," said Jim, "made my trip, more than a day's limit of ducks."

BEWICK'S SWAN AND JANKOWSKI'S: ONE SWAN OR TWO?

Question: What do Leo, Stella, Tangey, Bitsa, Nebula, Hazel, and Zodiac all have in common? The answer: They are seven of the identifying names the Wildfowl and Wetlands Trust in England has given to its population of migratory Bewick's Swans (*Cygnus columbianus bewickii*)

Each wild swan flying in to Slimbridge has been identified by the Trust, and their personalized names, together with the careful drawing of their heads, front, sides, and lower bill, appeared as "cover" swans on the seventeenth *Annual Report of the Wildfowl Trust* (*1964–65*).

To accomplish this feat of swan naming took an artist's eye and a naturalist's keenness, a happy combination of talent which exists in artist/naturalist Sir Peter Scott, founder of the Wildfowl and Wetlands Trust at Slimbridge, England. Here it was discovered that the Bewick's Swan's bill bears a yellow mark as unique to each swan as a human thumbprint, and a swan arriving at Slimbridge could be observed and each individual clearly identified. As the

Variations in bill-markings of
Bewick's Swans (Derived from a
drawing by Sir Peter Scott)

Wildfowl Trust grew, and the detailed drawings of Bewick's Swans multiplied, Scott (whom you met earlier, painting the Whoopers at the edge of the marsh) was aided in his work by his family, his wife Philippa and their daughter Dafila, as well as a staff of trained naturalists who gravitated to the Trust like the wild swans. The study of Bewick's Swans by the Trust is arguably the most definitive cataloging of wild swans — and possibly of wildfowl species — ever undertaken.

The Bewick's has a range almost as far-flung as its fellow Arctic and Eurasian swan, the Whooper, extending from Western Europe to the Far East of China and Japan. (I say almost as far-flung because I have finally reached the point where I must face another taxonomic puzzlement in my naming of the swans of the world.)

The Bewick's has a look-alike which has been given a separate species or subspecies classification and name (depending on who is doing the classifying and naming). It is the Jankowski's Swan (*Cygnus columbianus jankowskii*, Alpheraky). If you're in the hair splitters camp, you will say there are nine swan species of the world, and you will insist that the Jankowski's Swan belongs in the ninth place.

The Jankowski's is said to winter in Japan, China, and Korea, and the Bewick's in Britain and northern Europe. The breeding range of the Bewick's extends over northern Russia from the Kanin Delta to the Lena Delta of Siberia, and the Jankowski's breeding range is from the Lena Delta to the Kolymia Delta. The Bewick's is claimed as a European swan, and the Jankowski's as an Asian swan. It is also called the Eastern Bewick's.

The distinction between the two swans is slight, but again, the identification of the two rests chiefly with the appearance of the bill. Each swan (like the Whooper, Tundra, and Trumpeter) is all white feathered, straight necked, and each, like Whooper and Tundra, has a black bill with a small yellow marking. Each swan, Bewick's and Jankowski's, is smaller than the Whooper. Indeed, one classification for the Bewick's has been *Cygnus minor*, "lesser swan," to distinguish it from the Whooper, a much larger swan.

But the main distinction between Jankowski's and Bewick's is that the Bewick's has a smaller less full bill, and the Jankowski's with the larger bill has a slightly longer neck.

Now if you lump the two swans together and you merge their two ranges, as most scientists now do, with winters for the Bewick's in Britain and winters for the Jankowski's in Japan, you still will not come up with a total range as large in area as the Whooper's which extends from Iceland to Japan.

If you're out in that snowy field, like Peter Scott in Britain or Teiji Saga in Japan, you will hear a decidedly different call, distinguishing the Bewick's/Jankowski's from the Whooper.

When nature writer Louis J. Halle listened to the Bewick's calling one cold day in late fall as they landed in a Dutch field he responded to their high pitched sound and characterized it as "heavenly music."

The Bewick's Swans which Halle had come upon are thought to belong to over half the western population which winters in the Netherlands. Halle was witnessing a score land on the island of Texel off the Dutch coast:

October 21, 1972, on the island of Texel
off the Dutch Coast, over twenty Bewick's
Swans, which had arrived in the preced-
ing few days were feeding or sleeping in a
field. The spectacle was extraordinarily
beautiful because the sun was shining
and the swans were in a flock of grazing
widgeon that surrounded them on all
sides and were interspersed among them.
The contrast between the great size and
whiteness of the swan, and the small
ducks like wildflowers, gave a celestial
splendor to the scene.

Suddenly there was heavenly music from
the air and from the ground alike. They
were singing as they sank through the
air, and the swans on the ground, lifting
their heads, were also singing to greet

113

them. The four, feet extended, dropped lightly to the ground in the midst of the others, just as geese do when they land in a field. *(The Appreciation of Birds)*

Halle's description of the swans singing as they sank through the air is reminiscent of American ornithologist Daniel Girard Elliott's famous description of the swan calling at death which is, as far as I am aware, the only modern report of the swan song. Elliott shot one in Currituck Sound over a century ago (mentioned earlier).

Peter Scott, who has listened to hundreds of Bewick's and to hundreds of Whoopers as well, compared the two calls of larger and lesser swans by attributing the higher pitched call to the Bewick's, and he notes that the Bewick's has a less resonant call than the Whooper.

The difference between Whooper and Bewick's together with the establishment of the Bewick's as a distinct species was made in 1830 by ornithologist William Yarrell, who also gave the smaller swan its taxonomic description in honor of Thomas Bewick, engraver and ornithologist, who had died two years before.

But it was left to Peter Scott and the Wildfowl Trust to pursue the most thorough investigation and study of a swan species ever possible.

As in all great endeavors, particularly when careful research is involved, the observation and study of the swans and the total population of Bewick's as well, started small and grew large. The Wildfowl Trust was established at Slimbridge, England, as the Severn Wildfowl Trust in 1946, a year after World War II, when ornithologists and aviculturists all over the world were beginning to return to the cultivation of wildfowl after the decimation and sometimes total destruction of their waterfowl collections during the wounded planet's war years. In France, Jean Delacour had to start over completely to restore his carefully managed waterfowl collection which was wiped out by the war.

In 1946 the Bewick's did not, according to Peter Scott, habitually land in the enclosures at Slimbridge, but a captive pair of North American Tundra Swans (*Cygnus columbianus columbianus*) living at Slimbridge "pursuaded the wild Bewick's to land."

THE
WILDFOWL
& WETLANDS TRUST

Scott's Tundras at Slimbridge are American swans, very close in size and marking to the Bewick's, so close that the American Ornithologists' Union considers the two a single species. The paradox here lies not just with their conspecificity but with their name. The Tundra bears the name *columbianus*, a distinctly American name to indicate its habitat near the Columbia river in Oregon. Thus the British Bewick's (pronounced, incidentally, like the American motor car Buick) flies around with an American appellation as does the Jankowski's which also bears *columbianus* in its descriptive species name — each swan far from the Oregon River. To this date, according to Greenwall's *First Breedings of Wild Wildfowl in North America*, neither Bewick's nor Jankowski's has been successfully bred in North America.

But Peter Scott did breed the Bewick's successfully in England. A mate for a solitary male was acquired from Holland and they bred. This was the first time, Scott believes, a wild pair of Bewick's was bred in captivity. The female, Mrs. Noah, lived a long and productive life at Slimbridge, residing there for thirty-two years, and she died of old age in 1982 after producing a total of 159 eggs of which thirty-nine hatched and twenty-seven were successfully reared.

The Bewick's dynasty established by Mrs. Noah drew wild migrating Bewick's and by 1964/65, when the naming classification of each individual swan was well underway, over thirty pairs

were wintering at the Wildfowl Trust. In one extremely cold winter, the wild swans numbered almost 725.

To endow an animal with its given name, not merely a common or species name but a personal and individual name such as my own dog's name, Bala, or a friend's dog, Ciaro, personalizes and creates an attachment, a bond which every farmer and rancher knows — and generally avoids if they are raising animals for food.

Thus each Bewick's from the "foundation swans," Mrs. Noah and her mate, up to the entire flock of wild Bewick's were given individual names, frequently names which suited their "swan personality." This was possible only because the yellow marking on the bill is unique to the individual swan. By 1965, when the cover swans appeared on the *Wildfowl Trust Annual Report*, a daily register was kept on each swan. Their arrivals and departures were noted on the register, and careful colored drawings made of the bill: front, sides, and lower views. Even the sex — not easy to determine in swans — was recorded without, as Scott remarks, "too many errors."

As with all detailed research, sometimes the future use and value of the research might not be known at the time it is initiated. In 1986, Slimbridge was asked to determine if the Bewick's swans who summer in Russia carried radiation levels from the nuclear accident at Chernobyl. Birds were captured and the radiation measure in each individual checked. "Happily," says Scott, "the sensitive machine" used to record the levels "found only background radiation in the swan."

However, the careful study of radiation gave some new information of the Bewick's examined. It was discovered that thirty-four percent carried lead shot in the tissue. One swan was found to have "twenty-one pellets of three different shot sizes." Lead shot in the tissues will not necessarily kill a bird. However, that such a heavy concentration of pellets was found in the swans says something about hunting in the countries through which the Bewick's pass, for the swans are protected in all of the countries in their range.

Lead shot in the tissue of a bird may not be life threatening, but when spent lead shot is ingested by a swan from the river bottoms where it feeds, death is nearly certain. The Mute Swan living its traditional life on the Thames River has been severely threatened by hunter's lead shot and the fisherman's lead weights.

But even with pellets in the tissues, the hardy Bewick's survived a round trip to Britain from the Russian breeding ground and back — over 4,600 miles. The Bewick's have continued to flourish (so far), and the population has grown to an estimated 16,500.

When an arm of that world population of Bewick's migrates to Slimbridge — or Welney or Martin Mere, all places in England where the Wildfowl and Wetlands Trust has extended its own range — the swans flying in are not merely strange and beautiful creatures arriving like sudden gods from a mythic realm, they are old familiars. They are returnees with names like Lancelot and Prongy, old-timers who have been repeat arrivers for more than a score of years. Thus the Bewick's swans come to the Wildfowl and Wetlands Trust each fall to find there a safe haven — a "local habitation and a name."

The Wildfowl & Wetlands Trust's Centres

CAERLAVEROCK ●   ● WASHINGTON

CASTLE ESPIE ●

● MARTIN MERE

● WELNEY

LLANELLI ●

● SLIMBRIDGE

● ARUNDEL

THE TUNDRA SWAN: A WHISTLER

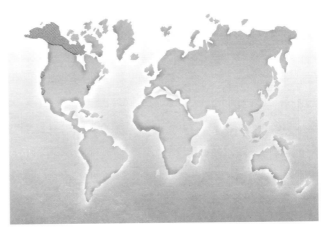

\When explorers Merriweather Lewis and William Clark, aided in their journey by Native American Sacajawea, were trekking up the Missouri River and then westward to the Pacific Ocean on their famous expedition of 1806, they kept many records, bringing back reports which opened American eyes to vast new knowledge of the fauna existing in the unexplored regions of the continent.

On their journey through the wilderness they noted down and distinguished the strange calls of the two American swans. From the lesser swan, they heard a kind of whistling sound, a call which "terminates in a round full note, louder at the end." Thus, as they listened and recorded their observations, Lewis and Clark endowed the smallest of the two American swans with its common name: the Whistling Swan (Banko).

The name seemed appropriate to the swan, and it still may be found in field guides written by numerous authorities. In 1983, however, the American

Ornithologists' Union voted to change the name Whistling to Tundra Swan. Therefore, *Cygnus columbianus*, identified by Ord in 1815, presents a problem not only at the species level (with the lumpers who insist that it and the Eurasian Bewick's are one species), but also at the vernacular level when the swan's common name is used.

The A.O.U. had a procedure behind their name change; the new name designates the tundra area of the far North American Arctic where the swan breeds. A parallel to this exists in the Latin descriptive name of species *columbianus*. It is also geographical and designates the Columbia River area in Oregon where the western population winters and where Lewis and Clark discovered the swan and took note of it.

The first breeding pair of Tundras which I have ever witnessed, I saw at Kortright Waterfowl Park (named for gamehunter and writer Francis Kortright) near Guelph, Ontario, Canada. It was the end of July — chilly enough for visitors to wear sweaters. The park lay in that steep Canadian silence of wood and pond where white-tailed deer flick away the shadows of the afternoon. I rounded a corner of a path through dense wood and beheld the two swans with their solitary adolescent cygnet loafing on the bank. When the adults caught sight of me, someone they took to be a stealthy intruder, they began their twinned warning call, a chorus of EE-EE-YOW! EE-EE-YOW! Like their closely related fellows, the four northern swans, they acted in concert by stretching their necks straight out for the call, then ended, still mirror images of one another, by pointing their heads downward, a posture called ground-staring, which is a characteristic finale to a threat display of the Arctic swans.

The cygnet between them appeared to be in a drowsy reverie, very much like a human adolescent boy or girl who thinks: why are my parents making all that fuss? But the parents kept up their warning, and somehow or other they marshaled their child to his/her reluctant webbed feet and sailed off into the water. The three headed away from my intrusion. Still calling, they persisted long enough for me to hear them quite plainly, but they were far enough away to be out of focus for my long-range camera lens.

Though not often found in captivity, and Kortright Park's Niska Foundation is credited as one of the first to breed Tundra in captivity, this pair had obviously been raised successfully in the Waterfowl Park. They were, no doubt, accustomed to park naturalists and to visitors, but the pair exhibited all the wary acumen of the truly wild — no doubt a trait which has saved them over the centuries from the severe decimation of North American commercial hunting.

Breeding high up near the Arctic Circle and wintering on the Atlantic prong of the eastern flyway to North Carolina and on the Pacific side to Oregon, the Tundra is a certifiably northern swan. A hundred years ago it ranged in great numbers as far south as the Gulf Coast of Texas. The great flocks have vanished there now, but a few casuals are reported from time to time. The Tundra, flying at levels reported to be as high as 8,000 feet, has escaped the decimation suffered by the larger American, the Trumpeter.

Despite its high flight pattern and its wariness, the Tundra has suffered incidents of terrible slaughter. In 1880, George B. Sennett reported in the "Bulletin of the Nuttall Ornithology Club" that wholesale devastations of a Tundra flock occurred in Pennsylvania, the same state where flocks of Tundra

120

stop off on a stage of their long migration.

Bennett writes: "Such a catastrophe occurred to the flocks of Northwestern Pennsylvania on March 22, 1879. Swans came down in many places in four counties in ponds, streams, fields or villages. Large numbers were killed by men and boys with guns, rifles, and clubs. Twenty-five were captured alive in one village, as they were worn out and helpless after their battle with the storm. Most of those that alighted within sight of human habitation were slaughtered wantonly" (quoted by Edward Howe Forbush in *Birds of America*).

Long before Europeans settled on this continent, the Native Americans could look up in the skies and see thousands upon thousands of great birds — among them the Tundra and Trumpeter Swans. On the Great Seal of the Chickasaw Nation, adopted in 1867, stands the War Chief Tishomingo. In the words of the Chickasaw, he is the "last battle chief of the Chickasaw Tribe. He stands in the manner of peace, and he carries his weapons to demonstrate his ability and willingness to defend his people. The feathers in his hair and adorning his shield are those of the swan. Swans, noted for their grace and tenderness with their young, were treated with respect and admiration by the Chickasaw people" (From the publication "Welcome to the Chickasaw Nation").

The Great Seal of the Chickasaw Tribe

The Chickasaw and Osage tribes of the south and southwest were not alone in their reverence for the swan. In the north, the Chippewa (or Ojibway) Tribe who settled on the shores of Lake Superior, "the shining big sea water" of the *Song of Hiawatha* poem, had a long tradition of veneration for the swan's magical powers in their folklore and myth.

Henry Wadsworth Longfellow based most of his narrative poem of the epic hero Hiawatha on the writing and research of early ethnographer Henry Rowe Schoolcraft's *Algic Researches: Indian Tales and Legend*. Married to a Native American wife, Schoolcraft took down and published the many northern Indian stories.

Longfellow, who received a great deal of critical cant for his poem — so much so that fellow greats like Nathaniel Hawthorne and Ralph Waldo Emerson stepped forward to champion the work — gave full credit to

The Son of the Evening Star

Can it be the sun descending

O'er the level plain of water?

Or the Red Swan floating, flying,

Wounded by the magic arrow,

Staining all the waves with crimson,

With the crimson of its life-blood,

Filling all the air with splendor

With the splendor of its plumage?

Henry Wadsworth Longfellow
from *Song of Hiawatha*, Part XII

Schoolcraft's *Algic Researches*, saying clearly that the stories of Indian legend were a major source for Hiawatha. However, the meter or rhythm of the poem was modeled on the Finnish folk epic the "Kalevala," compiled by Lönrot. In the Finnish poem, swans also figure strongly as creatures of magic and beauty with the same charmed quality which makes them impervious to the hunter's arrow as in the American Indian legend.

Longfellow included the original Ojibway story as Schoolcraft related it in a footnote to the "Red Swan" passage (the passage which appears at the beginning of this section on the Tundra Swan). Schoolcraft's story reveals quite clearly the reverence in which the Ojibway held the swans, once so numerous on the Great Lakes. In a considerably shortened version, this is the way the story goes:

"There were once three brothers," who made a wager as to who would bring in the first game. Their bargain was that they would shoot no other animal but the one that each brother was accustomed to hunt. With that as the rule of the wager, the three hunters set out in different ways.

The youngest brother Odjibwa first encounters a bear, an animal he is not to kill by the agreement. But Odjibwa breaks his word and kills the bear, contrary to his bet.

Suddenly something red tinges the air around him. He rubs his eyes thinking he has been tricked, then he hears what he takes to be a human voice. He is curious and he follows the voice until he reaches the lake. There he sees the prize for which he is searching.

At a distance out on the lake floats a most beautiful Red Swan, whose plumage glitters in the sun and who makes the strange human noise he had followed. Odjibwa sneaks up to be within bow-shot and takes aim.

The arrow strikes, but apparently takes no effect, for the swan continues to swim around and to dip its head as if all the arrows Odjibwa shoots at it have no effect.

The young hunter runs home to get all his arrows and his brothers' arrows as well. He returns to the lake and fires a barrage of arrows at the swan who seems totally unharmed.

Odjibway remembers that his deceased father has left a medicine sack with three magic arrows. Again Odjibway returns home, this time to get the three magic arrows which he knows he is forbidden to touch.

But Odjibway caught up in the excitement of the great prize "seizes the magic arrows and runs back to the shore." The Red Swan is still there, and he shoots the first magic arrow with great precision. The arrow comes very near the swan. The second arrow comes still closer. When he takes the last arrow from the quiver, he feels his arm grow firmer, and he draws the bow string with great strength. The arrow pierces the neck of the swan a little above the breast. But even wounded, the bird begins to fly away. At first it flies slowly, flapping its wings and rising gradually, then it flies off toward the sinking sun.

Longfellow ends his passage of the Red Swan with:

> Yes; it is the sun descending,
> Sinking down into the water;
> All the sky is stained with purple,
> All the water flushed with crimson!
> No; it is the Red Swan floating,
> Diving down beneath the water;
> To the sky its wings are lifted
> With its blood the waves are reddened!

Since those changed beings, the earliest civilized human (*Homo sapiens sapiens*) began to draw on the walls of caves to depict the animals which they both hunted and revered, the bird, and in particular the swan, has been a "symbol of transcendence," a link between the earthbound human and the upper world, a realm of mystery, the place which some of us call heaven.

Mythologist Joseph Campbell pointed out the Paleolithic cave painting in Lascaux, France; "There is a shaman depicted lying in a trance wearing a bird mask with a figure of a bird perched on a staff behind him." At Cahokia Mounds near St. Louis, Missouri, site of a later (750 A.D.) Native American culture, now vanished, not only the hollow bones of swans were found by archeologists, but the artifact of a half-bird, half-man was discovered carved in stone. Another message of primal man's honor and respect for the "transcendent" image of the bird.

Certainly the Hiawatha poem and the Ojibway legend from which it

Birdman Tablet
Sandstone tablet depicting a man in bird costume and mask
Cahokia Mounds

draws reveal that, like European man, the Native American had a tradition of spiritual regard for birds such as the swans.

The human of the Ojibway story, one of the three hunter brothers is a deceitful being, a hunter who breaks a vow to his own brothers and then, so eager for the prize of the Red Swan, commits the outrage of stealing his dead father's magic arrows so that he may kill the bird of sunset whose purity makes it impervious to his arrows.

Coincidentally (and an expert mythologist and folklorist such as Joseph Campbell might point to a deep link here, a universal symbol which Jungians call an archetype) in *The Kalevala*, a compilation of the Finno-Ugria race's tales put in the form of an epic poem, there is also the element of a reckless, overly proud human, Lamminkainen, the hunter who travels to the entrance of Tuonela the kingdom of the dead following "the long-necked bird" he wishes to slay. Because Lamminkainen does not know the magic words to save him from his act, he is thrown into the depth of the "black-billowed" river and torn to pieces by the blood-stained son of the underworld King Tuoni (*Larousse Mythology*).

This great saga was transformed into music by the Finnish composer Jan Sibelius as the "Swans of Tuonela" inspired not only by the Finnish epic but by the actual swans, flying outside his window and landing on a little Finnish Lake. Today, the swan (a Whooper) is the national bird of Finland.

As is evident from the 1879 incident in Pennsylvania and other recorded present-day tragedies, some — certainly not all — modern hunters have occasionally ignored the deep-seated taboo on killing the swan, a taboo passed down in legend from many areas of the world. Because the Tundra Swan is still populous (170,000— although John Terborgh made a compilation of bird counts showing the Tundra population on Chesapeake Bay decreased 27 percent from 1950 to 1980), the swan may still be legally hunted in six of the fifty United States. The states which allow hunting lie on both arms of the Tundra migration and the Tundra migrates farther than all swans, covering up to 4,000 miles.

To the east, hunting of the swan is permitted in Virginia and North Carolina. The Swan Research Program at Airlie, Virginia under the direction of Dr. William Sladen is "strongly opposed to the hunting of swans and has called out for support from citizens to stop the hunting of this elegant ambassador of the wetlands," which, as Dr. Sladen points out, "is enjoyed by far more people than a handful of hunters." In the west, hunting is legal in Montana, Nevada, North Dakota, and Utah. The western states' area of Tundra hunting overlaps the population of the endangered look-alike: the Trumpeter.

Because the Tundra, all white feathered but much smaller, may be confused with the Trumpeter, some hunters do not refrain from shooting the rare Trumpeter right out of the sky.

Aware of this, the National Trumpeter Swan Society, a society composed chiefly of scientists who are working desperately to save and even to restore the larger American swan, puts out posters warning hunters of the similarity of the two swans who at a distance might be confused one from the other.

In their publication "Swan Identification," the society puts the differences quite succinctly, also including the Mute Swan which has gone wild in some states:

Trumpeter Swan Society logo

Appearance

Tundra: black bill, usually with yellow spot varying size in front of the eye; this spot may be absent in some Tundras.

Trumpeter: black bill with red border on lower mandible; the red border may be present on some Tundras.

Mute: orange with prominent black knob at the base.

Voice
an absolute method of species identification.

Tundra: high-pitched, often quavering OO-OO-OO accentuated in the middle; or Who, Who-Ho; Woo-oo-woo or Who-who.

Trumpeter: resonant sonorous, loud, low-pitched, buglelike call

Mute: generally silent but not "mute;" hissing sounds are common.

Even with all the society's work, the rare Trumpeter has not escaped death from hunters, although the society does not take an "antihunting" stance.

Those who kill swans do not always go totally free from public outcry. In 1988, an incident was reported from Kalamazoo, Michigan when two Western Michigan University football players were charged with ripping off the head of a campus swan. The judge in the case was inundated with letters protesting the killing. Kalamazoo District Judge James Coyle reported that he had received more letters on the "swan case" than any other case that had come before him in his eight years on the bench, letters which were "unanimously pro-swan." A campus group put out a poster bearing the message, "Save the Swan — Drown a Football Player" (Associated Press release in *South Haven*, Michigan *Tribune*, May 5, 1988).

The reaction to the random killing of the campus swan and the resultant "pro-swan" outcry is a sign — one incident among many, but evidence of a growing awareness in America and in the world of the necessity to protect our wildfowl, indeed our wild fauna of all species.

Scientists say the Tundra arrived in the twentieth century still numerous, despite incidents such as the one in Pennsylvania, primarily because its habits differ from the endangered Trumpeter Swan. First of all, the Tundra breeds much farther north than the Trumpeter, and second, because it is smaller it was not desired as a swanskin by commercial hunters as was the Trumpeter.

A. M. Bailey, an early swan watcher, reported that the Tundra has a habit of arriving early in the north such as Alaska and arctic Canada. He says the Tundra "owe their present-day numbers to the fact that they nest over a wide stretch of barren country, uninhabited even by natives. They are continually persecuted on their breeding ground, and were it not for their habit of nesting early, when the snow is deep and too soft for travelling, they would have been exterminated long ago" (from Kortright quoting Bailey).

Not only does the Tundra differ from the Trumpeter and other waterfowl in its early arrival at the breeding grounds, but it has been a bird which frequents salt marshes and estuaries rather than inland fresh water as is the Trumpeter's choice.

But fresh water can be a choice for the Tundra. Dayton O. Hyde was rewarded one day after his and his family's enormous efforts to put in a lake on the site of a prehistoric lake with the arrival of a family of Tundras:

"One day as I sat at the listening point in front of the cabin, wishing for a cloud burst, I heard a mournful whoop from the gray scudding clouds. For a moment the mists opened as for an angel and the sun's rays made a golden stairway down the land. Down that stairwell glided five great white whistling swans. Circling the lake they whooped in apparent disbelief that such a body of water could exist" (Hyde).

Perhaps it takes people like Hyde who will make a herculean effort to create new wetlands and ponds for waterfowl. But it also takes Hyde's willingness to be silent and to listen to the silence for such a rewarding sight. And because there are people such as Hyde and William Sladen it is still possible for some of us to behold such a wonder and hear like Lewis and Clark heard in the early wilderness, that still pristine call, that "loud full note."

THE TRUMPETER SWAN: A SHINING MARK

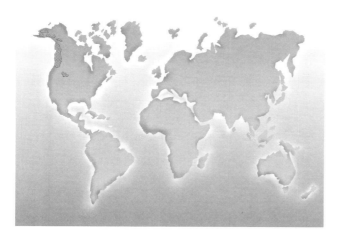

"I had lived to be nearly fifty years old before I saw my first wild swan," wrote Arthur Cleveland Bent seventy years ago. "It was a sight worth waiting for, to see a flock of these magnificent, great snow-white birds, glistening in the sunlight against the clear blue sky, their long necks pointing northward toward their polar home, their big black feet trailing behind, and their broad translucent wings slowly beating the thin upper air as they sped onward in their long spring flight."

Thus A. C. Bent began the section on "Swans of North America," a part of his twenty-volume study *Life Histories of North American Birds*, a classic work so important that it has remained in print since 1925, published by Dover Books. At the time Bent wrote the passage on swans he was introducing the Tundra Swan and not the Trumpeter. Devoted ornithologist and field naturalist that he was, A. C. Bent could hold out little hope to his readers that even the most diligent birder would ever see a Trumpeter Swan, much less behold an entire flock on seasonal migration.

The Trumpeter, the largest swan in North America, indeed the largest swan in the world, had been numerous during the time Audubon watched them flock in Kentucky, and since that time "systematically exterminated by hunting" — hunting engaged in primarily for commercial gain, but sport hunting as well (Banko). As another contemporary ornithologist Edward Howe Forbush warned, "trumpetings that were once heard the breadth of the continent as the long converging lines drove from zone to zone, will soon be heard no more."

By the 1930s, ornithologists thought the Trumpeter to be near extinction. And so it was. Once so populous on the North American continent that it was a familiar on the Atlantic seaboard, the Central Plains in Texas, and the Pacific Coast, by 1932 ornithologists counted only sixty-six Trumpeters inhabiting a narrow area (in comparison to their former range) near the Yellowstone. It was the last stronghold where the swans could survive through severe winters helped by the warm geothermal pools which provided constant open water.

To write his section on the Trumpeter which followed the section on the Tundra, A. C. Bent could not send out a call for field reports from naturalists as was his habit in dealing with each species of waterfowl. He had to rely on the reports made by John James Audubon seventy years before his own time and who felt "their geographical range to be an unsolved problem" (Audubon, *The Birds of America*).

"The Trumpeter," wrote Bent sadly, "belongs to a vanishing race." Once so far flung throughout North America, "it now probably does not breed anywhere within the limits of the United States, except possibly in some of the wilder portions of Montana and Wyoming; civilization has pushed it farther and farther north until now it is making its last stand in the uninhabited wilds of North Canada" (Bent).

That Trumpeters have survived to this day as a species is a near miracle — a result of the hard work on the part of naturalists who have watched over and protected the swan in the wild and who continue to engage in active breeding programs of captive birds. But most importantly, naturalists have fought for legislation to protect the swans, a battle which is going on today.

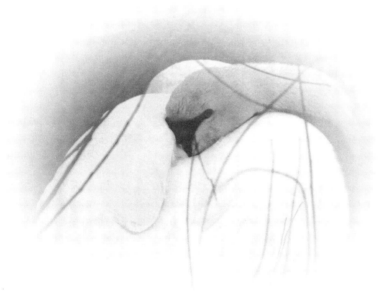

That this species could become extinct, that from great plenitude its numbers could drop exponentially until the last of the species died and its "beauty," as Miriam Rothschild says, is "gone forever", became a real and clear possibility to ornithologists of the early twentieth century who stood by and watched the death of the last Passenger Pigeon, Martha, dying in the Cincinnati Zoo in 1914, and the last Carolina Parakeet in 1918.

The notion of the extinction of a species, when looked at through history's lens, is a comparatively new one. It all began with two scientists, both of whom were born in 1769 and died in the 1830s. Each was a mere boy when Carolus Linnaeus died, but their combined work, in the words of Loren Eisely, "greatly improved the taxonomical classifications of animals." Their work might be said to be "symbiotic," for each influenced the other (Eisely, "The Pirate Chart").

It was up to the first of the two scientists, William Smith, to begin reading and interpreting geological strata and to the second, Baron Georges Cuvier, "the magician of the charnal house," to put the bones of vertebrates found in the strata together into an entire animal such as the lordly extinct Pterodactyl, the Mesozoic era flying reptile.

Had it not been for these two discoverers, humans might very well have gone along their way trodding haphazardly on the very earth which held entire histories of extinct life, unaware that fabulous animals such as the extinct dinosaurs once existed on the planet.

Armed with this fearful knowledge of extinction, aware of species disappearing in the past and from their own living world, nineteenth-century naturalists united into the American Ornithologists' Union and into the Audubon Society. Through their efforts on May 7, 1894, the Lacey Act was passed in Congress which established wildlife protection in Yellowstone Park, home of the Trumpeter and other disappearing animals such as the Bison. A second Lacey Act was passed in 1900, but its protection did not prevent the near extirpation of the Trumpeter. However, nineteen years later, naturalists discovered there were indeed a few pairs of Trumpeter still nesting in the Park. The swans owed their existence to the Lacey Acts' protection.

Just prior to the discovery of the nesting Trumpeters, the Weeks McLean Law was passed in 1913, and a major step toward preservation of Tundras and Trumpeters was made with the Migratory Bird Treaty Act of 1918. This treaty mandated a "closed" season on both species of native North American swans for the first time. Consequently, there was a slim chance that Trumpeters surviving outside the protection of Yellowstone Park might be protected from the double-barreled shotguns which "volleyed and thundered" throughout the mountains and valleys of the Trumpeter's home.

In the year of the crash on Wall Street, 1929, the Migratory Bird Conservation Act authorizing acquisition of land for waterfowl refuges was passed by Congress. When the Act was ultimately funded in 1934, the Red Rock Lake Migratory Refuge was established in Montana. The last stronghold of the Trumpeters was finally protected.

Even after forty years of progressive legislative acts had ensured a small island of safety for the Trumpeter Swan, the battle was by no means won and continues today. The Trumpeter Swan Society, meeting in 1991 in Utah, discussed the problem of continued legal hunting of the Trumpeter's sibling swan the Tundra in such states as Utah and even Montana. Thus, the Trumpeter and the smaller Tundra are yet "shining marks" for sportsmen in the west of the United States — and east where the Tundra also migrates.

This is what Edward Howe Forbush said eighty years ago:

> A swan seen at any time of the year in
> most parts of the United States is the sig-
> nal for every man with a gun to pursue
> it. . . .
>
> The swan lives to a great age. The older
> birds are about as tough and unfit for
> food as an old horse. Only the younger
> are savory, and the gunners might well
> have spared the adult birds but it was a

"sport" to kill them and fashion called for swansdown. The large size of this bird and its conspicuousness have served as in the case of the Whooping Crane, to make it a shining mark.

Alexander Pope
The Trumpeter Swan 1900
oil on canvas (56 ⅜ × 44 ⅜")
painting depicting dead Trumpeter
The Fine Arts Museums of San
Francisco, Museum purchase through
gifts from members of the Boards of
Trustees, The de Young Museum
Society and the Patrons of Art and
Music, Friends of the Museums, and by
exchange, Sir Joseph Duveen, 72.28

Just as I finished writing out Forbush's words, almost simultaneously with the last mark, came a lightning bolt outside on Lake Michigan, a sharp sound

132

like a giant shotgun going off just outside my window. Lake Michigan is rolling in, those quick undulating waves which can put any yachtsman to severe test, and may break a giant freighter in two. The Lake and sky seem filled with a frenetic rage, mirroring my own hopeless anger, as if to re-enforce the concept of the "pathetic fallacy", a literary notion of critics who accused poets of assuming nature to act in concert with the human being's every mood, desire, and need. Ben Johnson, Shakespeare's contemporary, took advantage of this idea in "To Penshurst" where fish and fowl present themselves rising up from water or falling from air in response to human need of fulfillment and plenty.

Once long ago, when I was camping out in the Camarque region of France on the banks of the Rhone River at the exact spot where Van Gogh painted fishing boats drawn ashore near Les Saintes Maries de la Mer, I awakened to the sound of gun fire volleying just outside my tent. Blam! blam! blam!

I looked out to see four French hunters clad in checked jackets firing away at a cloud of cranes hurrying toward Africa. Two of the birds fell into the Rhone River and were swallowed up at its confluence of the Mediterranean Sea. Hunting season had begun and a hunter's prize was captured by the sea. Ironically, it was here in the Camarque that Jean Delacour began his works of waterfowl conservation.

Not a hunter, or even one reared in a family of hunters (my father's idea of "roughing it" was to look for a golf ball in high grass), I have admittedly never truly understood that passionate moment of the kill. However, since the age of ten when I thumbed through the pages of *Field and Stream*, I have always had a respect for the true hunter and sportsman. It has been the wise hunters who have promoted the protection of wetlands and waterfowl. After all, it has been such hunters as Canadian Francis Kortright who promoted wildfowl protection. And one of the biggest lobbies for wetland protection has been the organization of hunters in "Ducks Unlimited," who, from the steamy course of the Deep Fork in Oklahoma to the cold zone of the Comox Valley in Canada, have worked to save wetlands and waterfowl.

I may not understand the hunter's mind or passionate drive for the kill, but, being human, I do understand the overwhelming drive to capture a prize,

The message of the Trumpeters will be repeated each time these wild calls echo across the United States and Canada. As they pass overhead, they will continue to remind us that wildlife's future lies in our own hands. We have choices and solutions.

Ruth Shea
Writing about the Trumpeter Swan, 1990.

a drive no doubt left over from our ancient hunter's brain. Go to an old-fashioned country fair and you will see the largest and the best capture the GRAND PRIZE, whether it be thousands of pounds of Hereford steer on the hoof or a 264-pound pumpkin from the pumpkin patch, it is they who win the purple rosette. Therein lies our own pathetic fallacy.

All animal species, whether predator or prey, are in their own manner hunters. Even if they are peaceful herbivores, the animal is hunting eternally for the best patch of grass, the largest and tastiest leaf.

The predator the American Bald Eagle is a true raptor, the consummate hunter in the air. On the ground in North America the four-footed predators are the near vanished wolf or the coyote. Each seizes the day and the prize, a law of nature. But animal species other than human search to spot the slow, the unwise prey. The mother Musk-ox who, terrified at a wolf attack, unwisely leaves her young calf to find protection in the phalanx of the herd, loses her calf to the wolf. Consequently, her genes are stopped in the mouth of the hunter.

Dayton O. Hyde is not only a hunter but a naturalist and conservationist. He understands how effective hunting up and down the food chain can create a balance of nature. When Hyde's Oregon ranch was plagued with gophers, and his neighbors were calling in crop-dusting planes like generals calling for air support, they spread poison pesticides over their own ranches and his. Angered, Dayton O. Hyde took a daring step forward into the past.

He allowed coyotes, indeed encouraged that rancher's bane, to live in harmony with cattle on the Hyde ranch. He did this, first of all, by seeing that the coyotes were well fed so they didn't go for his cattle. But the coyotes performed their job culling the gopher population, and they returned Hyde's ranch to the unpoisoned wilderness of old cowboy days.

In his book, *Don Coyote*, a recounting of his experience with coyotes, Hyde chronicles another experience of "watching the show of waterfowl on his lake" where "they draw together at an eagle's overhead passage as though they were trying to be single cells of a unit too large for an eagle to attack." Hyde thinks about the eagle who "picks up the sick and inept" and watching waterfowl and eagle he comes to a realization about hunted and hunters: "I realized for the first time how smoothly the system of predation must have worked for the health of all species before Man came along and dared Great Mother Nature as a fool.

"While the American Hunter, the sportsman, is only in the mildest sense selective, shooting the unwary, his tendency is to harvest the biggest most beautiful, making his selection on a visual basis rather than on a genetic one as other animals do, choosing the phenotype, [a type distinguished by individual appearance rather than by hereditary factors] — the genotype." In other words, the human predator goes for the trophy specimen, the strongest and the fleetest, whereas the animal predator goes for the easier catch, generally the cull, which is the weakest and slowest.

In the light of Hyde's words, it is easy to understand the continued decimation of the Trumpeter Swan population, the "biggest and most beautiful" of swans, a prize hunted commercially for its swanskins by the Hudson's Bay Company of trappers since the 1700s when they hunted the northern wilderness endowed with a charter from the Crown which gave them a dominion over the creatures of vast territory and the freedom to act, not like a business, but a nation.

When the commercial hunters were gone, they were replaced by sportsmen who aimed aloft at the few white brigades left in the sky — "sky-blasting" at the swans overhead.

Even after the establishment of the Red Rock Lake Refuge, the Trumpeter remained in jeopardy into the 1930s. "Later," says the Audubon Society, "since it was discovered that irresponsible waterfowl hunters were killing swans under the claimed pretext of shooting snow geese, the hunting seasons on snow geese were closed by counties in those states within the Trumpeter's breeding range; Idaho 1941, Montana 1942, Wyoming 1946. It took almost a half century before the Trumpeter was finally protected from guns. Even so the population remained endangered and it was put on the U. S. Government's Endangered List."

Since the earliest days of the explorers, Trumpeters had been reported in Alaska. However, according to James G. King writing in *Alaska Fish and Game*, "the first modern report was made in 1956 by Mel Manson who described nesting Trumpeters in the Copper River Canyon in Cordova [Alaska]. In 1959, U. S. Fish and Wildlife Service pilots counted 1,124 Trumpeters in interior south coast Alaska. In 1968, the first complete census was done by USFWS pilots. The survey disclosed an Alaskan population of 2,487. An additional 800 were tallied outside Alaska producing a total sufficient for the U. S. Government to remove them from the official 'Endangered Species List'" (IWWA Newsletter, Jan/Feb. 1988).

With the discovery of a relatively large population of Trumpeters in Alaska began media trumpetings heralding the success of the swan's survival, a brouhaha which James G. King found to be "after [Hans Christian Andersen's] tale of the 'Ugly Duckling,' the best known swan fable of today" (IWWA).

Despite valiant efforts coupled with legislation to protect this noble swan, the population is still unstable. No more is the Trumpeter seen plentiful and migrating over the shores of Gitchee Gumee, the "shining big sea water" of Longfellow's poem or for that matter over Ohio or Iowa. But the work of naturalists goes on and in 1984 what we have grown to term a "modern miracle" in our postmodern era, did occur — an occurrence which gave hope to all whose eyes are trained skyward in spring and fall.

The Trumpeters, long deemed "nonmigratory" because the resident population of the Yellowstone area are comparatively sedentary, migrated for the first time in over 100 years, and they were seen as far south as Oklahoma. The only wild North American swan I have ever seen in my home state (up until Russell and I saw the Trumpeters) was a Tundra Swan in the Center at the Chickasha National Recreation Park in central Oklahoma.

The Tundra I saw there stood wings raised in flight, its black feet pushing against the earth, a perpetual gesture frozen in time by the taxidermist's craft. Below the mounted swan the Park Naturalist had written, "This swan was shot near here. The person who shot it was apprehended by the Oklahoma Game Ranger and was fined $800."

If that statement wasn't enough to weigh heavily on any Nature Center goer, the naturalist added a quotation from S. Dillon Ripley, Secretary of the Smithsonian, now retired:

"To me the far-ranging Whistler [now called Tundra] swan has always seemed a perfect symbol of wilderness. They can be killed only illegally — and to what purpose? I feel only a fool would kill a swan, for to do so is to infringe on your birthright, to sully your natural surroundings, to scar your soul a little."

Certainly the killing of the Tundra Swan was and still is a scar on the American soul, but a greater, deeper one has been made by the killing of the rarer Trumpeter. That deep continental scar began to heal a bit when the Minnesota Trumpeters lifted off on migration.

From Minneapolis, Minnesota's Hennepin Parks, twenty-nine full-winged swans left Minnesota, travelled to Missouri, Kansas and Oklahoma where they remained for the winter. Of those twenty-nine swans, eighteen returned safely northward, according to Laurence Gillette of Hennepin Parks.

The migration of the Hennepin Parks swans was the first documented migration of the Trumpeter Swan in the lower forty-eight states in the past century. It showed in fact these birds "did still have the instinctive ability to enable them to migrate" (Nova, WGBH Transcript 1986).

Indeed the Trumpeter Swan was considered nonmigratory — too wary to traverse the United States. Because of this behavior, naturalists doubted that the offspring would ever migrate. But migrate they did, and it was from Hennepin Parks that the family of three Trumpeters came which my friend Russell and I saw on an Oklahoma lake in 1991.

The one step forward by the Hennepin swan migration has been a shining benchmark to naturalists. But it is not a final chapter of success. The Trumpeter Swan of the Yellowstone, the Rocky Mountain population, breed from an ever narrowing gene pool. Every spring new ways are searched for, and sometimes found, which enable the swans to procreate and to congregate in sufficient numbers in the Midwest that they might fly on migration, shining marks — a constellation of swans in the skies of North America.

*Where 15,630 Wild Trumpeter Swans
were counted in Summer 1990*

13,340
+41%

285
+102%

188
+150%

294
+203%

466
+41%

3
-50%

★ 12
+300%

3
-70%

28 ★
-27%

130
+18%

353
+18%

152
+245%

★ 60
-20%

58
+100%

★ 9
+100%

★ 12
-54%

★ 116
+40%

★ 6
+50%

Percents= Change since 1985
★ Starred populations= Introductions,
others are natural remnants

TRUMPETERS	1985	1990	% CHANGE
Alaska Population	9459	13,340	+41%
Wild Remnants other States	507	598	+18%
Wild Remnants Canada	649	1,236	+90%
★ Introduced Birds	283	456	+61%
In Captivity	551	893	+62%
Total World Population	11,449	16,523	+44%

Statistics obtained from the Trumpeter Swan Society.

Name	Habitat	Size	Clutch
Coscoroba *Coscoroba coscoroba*	South American: prefers coast to inland.	35 inches Cob: 10 lbs Pen: 8½ lbs smallest	4-7 creamy eggs Incubation 34-35 days
Black Necked *Cygnus melanocoryphus* also *Cygnus nigrocolis*	South American: prefers inland lakes. Floating nests. Spends most of life on water.	39 inches Cob: 12lbs Pen: 9 lbs (smallest of "True" Swans)	4-8 creamy eggs Incubation 35-37 days
Black *Cygnus atratus* also *Chenopis atratus*	Found on large, shallow lakes and swamps. A colonial nester.	46 inches Cob: 14 lbs Pen: 9 lbs	4-7 pale green eggs Incubation 35-37 days
Mute *Cygnus Olor* also *Sthenelides olor*	Rivers, lakes, reservoirs, ponds, sheltered coasts	59 inches Cob: 27lbs Pen: 30 lbs	4-8 greenish eggs Incubation 35-37 days
Bewick's *Cygnus columbianus bewickii* also *Cygnus minor*	Low marshy tundras, pools and lakes.	48 inches Cob: 14 lbs Pen: 13 lbs	4-6 white creamy eggs Incubation 31-33 days
Eastern Bewick's *Cygnus columbianus jankowskii*	Nests on small islands and rivers, esluaries, lakes or Tundra pools.	50 inches Cob: 15lbs Pen: 13 lbs	3-5 white creamy eggs
Whooper *Cygnus cygnus cygnus* (Linneaus) also *Cygnus musicus*	Tundra pools lakes, reservoirs and sea coasts.	60 inches Cob: 24 lbs Pen: 18 lbs	6-8 white creamy eggs Incubation 35-37 days
Tundra (Whistling) *Cygnus columbianus columbianus* also *Cygnus americanus*	Grassy lowland tundras, coasts	47 inches Cob: 18 lbs Pen: 14 lbs	Up to 7 white eggs Incubation 31-33 days
Trumpeter *Cygnus cygnus buccinator*	Pools and marshy ground; inland geothermal pools.	60 inches Cob: 28 lbs Pen: 23 lbs (largest)	4-8 white eggs Incubation 35-38 days

THE WORLD

Coloration	Voice	Range
Head, neck and body white. Wing tips black. Pinkish-orange bill. (The only swan feathered between bill and eye.)	Named cos-co-ro-ba by Tupi Indians. 4 notes loudly descending.	Extends from lower tip of South America north to lower Brazil. Greatest population: Chile and Argentina.
Black neck with white body. Red knob surmounts bluish-gray bill. Legs and feet pinkish. Yearling has black wing tips.	High pitched a kind of scree-ee. Also note that sounds like flute.	Breeds in southern third of South America and Falkland islands. May be found northward to tip southern of Brazil.
Blackish feathers with some brown. Red eye, red bill which is striped below nostril with white line, white wing tips.	A high pitched crooning call. Many conversational sounds.	Australia, New Zealand (introduced). Long thought non-migratory. Movement with rain fall. Dry years, clusters by sea.
All-white feathers. Bright orange bill surmounted by black knob. Black legs and feet (Royal). Polish sub-species pale legs and feet.	Called mute because it does not call. Bark-like mother call or conversational sound. Hiss	Resident in England, but migratory pockets across Europe/ Asia.
All white feathered with black bill and yellow patch on bill near eye. Patches so distinctive individual swans can be named.	Loud musical honk or goonk in flight: goo-a-loohk.	From north of Arctic Circle in Russia. Winters in northwestern Europe and England.
All white feathered with black bill, yellow marks. Distinguished from Bewick's only because of fuller bill		From north of Eurasian Arctic Circle, China, Japan and Korea.
All white feathered with black bill. Yellow patch near bill. Head appears triangular. Light around eye.	"Ang" hoop-hoop-hoop.	Across northern Eurasia from Iceland to Bering sea. Breeds in Iceland, Lapland, Russia, Asia.
All white feathered, black bill with small yellow patch. Sometimes no patch.	High pitched whistling sound: wow-wow-wow.	Arctic Alaska and northwest territories east to Hudson's Bay.
All white feathered. Black bill with Salmon red line at mandible.	Ko-hoh! A loud trumpeting sound.	Alaska to British Columbia Resident 4 corners of Montana, Idaho, Wyoming, Utah, (Yellowstone or Red Rock Lake.

John James Audubon, the Trumpeter Swan, and the Passenger Pigeon

Imagine...that a flock of fifty swans are thus

sporting before you... and you will feel as I have, more

happy and void of care than I can describe.

The 406th plate of John James Audubon's monumental work *Birds of America* depicts a Trumpeter Swan. Beneath the picture is the Latin name, *Olor buccinator*, followed, as is sometimes the custom, by the name of the individual who first gave the Latin descriptive name and thus first classified the creature. In this case, Sir John Richardson's name follows the Latin. It was Richardson who first positively distinguished the Trumpeter Swan from the only other native American swan, the much smaller Tundra Swan.

Yet even to those who are what Audubon called "closet naturalists," laboratory and book-bound investigators of nature rather than naturalists of the open field, it would be clear that the magnificent Trumpeter, the largest swan in the world, bears a stamp uniquely American, belonging to the great and richly abundant land that was once the North American continent.

Audubon reported seeing the Trumpeter Swan flocking by the hundreds, but he portrayed this individual bird as solitary, its neck bent back in a hairpin turn. The black beak open to snap at a moth reveals the distinctive salmon-colored line on the mandible, characteristic of the Trumpeter Swan.

As you look at this picture of the swan, you have the distinct impression that you are looking at it from the vantage point of another swan, possibly its mate. Certainly you are viewing the swan as if you were floating alongside it. You are so near, you can see a portion of the swan beneath the water. You can make out each detail of the black webbed foot as it strokes in a powerful back-

Trumpeter Swan
Cygnus buccinator
Engraving by John James Audubon

144

ward thrust. In the background, only a few clouds drift across the North American sky, a sky empty of birds.

That Audubon took a particular delight in this great swan species there can be no doubt. He once kept a wounded Trumpeter as a pet for "upwards of two years." Furthermore, he left most of the writing of the portion of his work devoted to the other native American swan, the Tundra Swan, to a Dr. Sharpless of Philadelphia. Audubon's focus was on the Trumpeter, and he wrote of the swan in one of the most lyrical of all passages in his works. To Audubon the swan was a bird "giddy with delight" until it heard the sound of his and his companion's guns.

While on a hunting expedition on rivers of Missouri and Kentucky, he writes of the Trumpeter: "To form a perfect conception of the beauty and elegance of these Swans, you must observe them when they are not aware of your proximity, and as they glide over waters of some secluded pond. . . . Imagine, Reader, that a flock of fifty Swans are thus sporting before you, as they have more than once in my sight, and you will feel, as I have, more happy and void of care than I can describe." At that time, Audubon could never have possibly imagined that by the turn of the century the sight of Trumpeters on the rivers of Missouri and Kentucky would have already vanished from the memory of the living.

Born in 1785 on the Island of Haiti, a son of a French Naval officer and Haitian mother, Audubon showed an early interest in drawing. It was not until after he came to the United States from France to flee conscription in the Napoleonic Wars that he embarked on several careers, some quasi-successful, one ending in bankruptcy when he was shot at for debt. His passion for birds resulted in that great and monumental work, *Birds of America*, a work of his drawings on 435 hand-colored folio plates issued in four volumes over a period of eight years (1827–1835) and accompanied by the texts *Ornithological Biography* in five volumes issued from 1831 to 1839.

Even today, when publishing art and nature books is a much easier process than it was in Audubon's time, the scope of his efforts and the research into field and forest to find specimens, let alone to draw them, to have the drawings executed by engravers, and to publish and distribute the finished books is an almost superhuman task, certainly an accomplishment which may only be called heroic.

To understand the age of Audubon, you must imagine an unexplored wilderness, thickets full of thousands of birds, a plentitude of nature that was overwhelming to the European settlers. Many species had never been classified by scientists; these were the ones Audubon called "Nondescripts" and which he was most eager to draw and to describe. With only brief experience as a taxidermist in a private natural history museum, he was treading on territory unimagined. He set out into the North American wilderness with a gun and a sketch book.

Modern birders and waterfowl artists have powerful binoculars through which they may watch from incredible distance the eye of a Pintail Duck turn in its head, but Audubon had no binoculars with which to study his subjects. He shot the birds down and then propped them up on wire armatures in likely poses, giving to them a lifelike rendering which stunned the world of his readers who would never see so many birds so accurately.

Many of the fine details of the Audubon's birds were executed with his favorite drawing instrument, the Trumpeter's pen feathers. His admiration for the beauty of the Trumpeter was only exceeded by his respect for the usefulness of its feathers, for he wrote that the Trumpeter quills which he used in drawing the feet and claws of many small birds were so hard, yet so elastic that the best steel-pen of his day (early 1800s) "might have blushed if it could be compared to them."

Audubon was not alone in admiring the feathers of the Trumpeter Swan. Desire for feathers and entire swanskins covered with feathers led to a wholesale slaughter of immense consequence. The Hudson's Bay Company, a British company trading in Canada since the 1630s, accounted for the demise of at least 94,326 swans, for that is the number of swanskins sold in England in that century of Audubon's lifetime. Adopting the Woodsman's stance of plainness toward European women of fashion, who he seems to believe engineered the entire massacre, he writes that he had seen these birds dying in agony, "their beautiful skins all intended for the ladies of Europe."

Hunting for sport was the privilege of the landed gentry. Americans, whose grandfathers had been constitutionally denied the right to hold noble titles, still enjoyed the "sport of nobles." Certainly the great plenty of the birds of America, for that matter all wildlife in North America, enticed subsistence hunters and commercial hunters onward through the marshes, the plains, and over the mountains, never thinking that the shots they fired took any effect in diminishing the great supply of animals in the wild continent so far west, yet so near to Eden.

Most early nineteenth century hunters' and woodsmen's thoughts went unrecorded, but John James Audubon's carefully detailed writings reveal man's relationship to that world of nature he was bent on conquering. Audubon's journals make a sometimes daily record of sightings and reveal much of his attitude and that of his fellows towards animals. "His pages," writes naturalist Edwin Way Teale, "present one of the clearest pictures we have of the attitude that prevailed in a period of age-old abundance" (Teale, *Audubon's Wildlife*).

Audubon reveals this abundance clearly when he goes along on a fur-trading expedition near the Tawapatee Bottom on the Mississippi, and becomes ice-bound with his partner Rozier and a party of hunters. It is then he records his impressions of the hundreds of Trumpeters he sees: "No sooner had the gloom of night become discernible through the grey twilight, the loud-sounding notes of hundreds of Trumpeters would burst on the ear; and as I gazed over the ice-bound river, flocks after flocks would be seen coming from afar and in various directions, and alighting about the middle of the stream opposite our encampment."

Not only had Audubon seen great flocks of Trumpeter Swans, even in his day an astonishing sight, but he watched thousands of Passenger Pigeons fly over as well, a sight common to most at that time. To illustrate their number in one passing alone, he made calculations which estimated that he saw "one billion one hundred and fifteen million, one hundred and thirty-six thousand pigeons in one flock."

The Passenger Pigeon (*Ectopistes migratorius*) is now extinct, the last one having died in the Cincinnati Zoo in 1914. It is considered by ornithologists to have been one of the most numerous species of all birds ever living in the recorded history of the world.

Passenger Pigeon
Columbiformes Columbidae Ectopistes Migratorius
Engraving by John James Audubon

147

Audubon saw the birds near Henderson, Kentucky, in such numbers that "the air was literally filled with pigeons; the light of noonday was obscured as by an eclipse; the dung fell in spots not unlike melting flakes of snow, and the continued buzz of wings had the tendency to lull my senses into repose."

Awareness of the destruction to the pigeons and swans was indeed "lulled into a repose." Although Audubon could calculate the billions of pigeons flying overhead in a single passage, he miscalculated the cumulative effect of hunting. He continually describes the wholesale slaughter of the Passenger Pigeons, not only on the occasion of their flight over Henderson, Kentucky, but at other killings. He reassures his readers with the comment that "on such occasions when the woods were filled with these pigeons they were killed in immense numbers, *although no apparent diminution ensues*" (emphasis mine).

The misperception that the killings of thousands of a species resulted in no harm to its abundance is the Catch-22 of the nineteenth-century mind, just as the twentieth-century mind misperceives the gradual effect of global warming. No one at that time, not even an Audubon, could possibly discern a pattern of destruction. However, on the other side of the globe in Europe, Baron Cuvier was just beginning to discover that whole species, such as the Pterosaur, had disappeared from the face of the earth, and poet Samuel Taylor Coleridge was writing of the Ancient Mariner who is cursed because he shoots the albatross, never to be freed of literally "wearing an albatross around his neck" until he gazes upon all God's creatures, including the "slimy" creatures of the deep, and "blesses them unaware."

In America, there were no boundaries a woodsman could perceive, no limit on the catch. A hunter, and Audubon was one of them, could take all he wished, leaving the wounded for other animals to devour. The animal kingdom was a rich kingdom and the endless land was the property of man, king of the animals.

When we read Audubon's words from our vantage point located in a world 150 years after his death, we look back knowing that shortly after his death in 1851, not only the Passenger Pigeon would become extinct in the 1900s, but the Great Auk (*Alka impennis*), The Labrador Duck (*Camptorhynchus labradorium*), and the Carolina Parakeet (*Cornuropsis carolinensis carolinensis*), all plen-

Detail of Audubon engraving
Great Auk
Charadriiformes Alcidae Pinguinus impennis

tiful in Audubon's day, would vanish from the North American continent, extinct before the turn of the nineteenth century. Furthermore, we know one of his favorites, the Trumpeter Swan, would be nearly extinct, biologists finding only sixty-six in the lower forty-eight states, and we find the view of the great ornithological artist and man of nature puzzling. It is as though we are watching a giant's shadow falling over a continent whose hero and champion, Audubon, is unaware of the approaching horror.

Artist and woodsman, John James Audubon is the image of not only the obvious genius, but of a great lover of nature, the biotic world. At the same time he is a perfect image of the ambiguity in human nature. "We are," says scholar Northrop Fyre, "fools of time." The heroic qualities of an Audubon place him above the normal limits of experience, but with the hero's magnificence which suggests something infinite, he is also imprisoned in the finite. In other words, though the hero, Audubon, may excel above all others giving a hint of the infinite, the nature of life is finite. Life ends in death. "There is nothing stranger," writes Charles Darwin not long after Audubon's own death, "than death of species."

Standing above his age, Audubon is (as are we all) still mired in it. He watches the destruction of the birds by his fellows with an ironic eye, and shares their attitude of play which can be shocking to those of us looking on from the twentieth century, ourselves "fools of time" who know the great contributions Audubon made to the preservation of bird species through the thousands of birders who followed in his name. In *Ornithological Biography* he writes of the "game" of Trumpeter Swan killing:

> One morning our men formed a plot
> against the swan, and having separated
> into two parties, one above, the other
> below them on the ice, they walked slowly,
> on a signal being given from the camp,
> toward the unsuspecting birds. Until the
> boatmen had arrived within a hundred and
> fifty yards of them, the swans remained as
> they were, having become, as it would

appear, acquainted with us, in consequence
of our frequently crossing the ice; but then
they all rose on their feet, stretched their
necks, shook their heads, and manifested
strong symptoms of apprehension. The
gunners meanwhile advanced, and one of
the guns going off by accident, the Swans
were thrown into confusion, and scamper-
ing off in various directions took to wing,
some flying up, some down the stream,
others making directly toward the shore.
The muskets now blazed and about a
dozen were felled some crippled, others
quite dead.

Audubon concludes this episode of the Trumpeter shooting with advice to
hunters: "I have been at the killing of several of these Swans, and I assure you
that unless you have a good gun well loaded with large buck-shot, you may
shoot at them without much effect, for they are strong and tough birds." If
Audubon had realized the cumulative effect of shooting the birds of America,
he certainly would not have thought the killing was "without much effect," nor
would he, upon gazing at the swans, have felt so rapturously "void of care."
"Audubon," writes Edward Way Teale, "misjudged the destructiveness of man."
But what Audubon saw and judged was a greater nemesis than hunting, a
nemesis we of this century now perceive as we view the shrinking wilderness
of the world.

Apparently the great woodsman could not see the harm the musket (its
name derived, in one of those little ironies of language, from the Latin for "little
fly") was wreaking on the bird populations. Audubon, however, was not totally
blind to the incursions of mankind. Because he was an artist and a hunter who
needed to shoot the birds for his drawings and for food, he seemed not to notice
the effect of the gun. Yet Audubon, not a farmer, saw clearly what the destruction of habitat by farmers was doing to avifauna in his own time in the destruction of wild plants, the birds' forage. He writes with alarm at the great stands of
cane vanishing: "The cane, kind reader, formerly grew spontaneously over the

great portions of the State of Kentucky and other western districts of our Union, as well as in many farther south. Now, however, cultivation, and introduction of cattle and horses, and other circumstances connected with the progress of civilization, have greatly altered the face of the country and reduced the cane within comparatively small limits."

Audubon was not entirely blind to the notion that a species could disappear when its habitat was destroyed. He gives an account of the slaughter of Passenger Pigeons by farmers, who at the pigeon's arrival in numbers "immense beyond conception, set to work knocking them out of trees with poles and burning them in pots of sulphur, lighted torches or shooting them down, until the final devastation and the hogs were let loose to feed on the dead and dying birds." It is then that Audubon gives us a hint that he considered the possibility that a species could die: "Persons unacquainted with these birds might naturally conclude that such dreadful havoc would soon put an end to the species. But I have satisfied myself, by long observation, that nothing *but the gradual diminution* of the forest could accomplish their decrease, as they not infrequently quadruple their numbers, and always at least double it" (emphasis mine).

To Roger Tory Peterson, artist/naturalist, and Virginia Peterson, who ponder the "Audubon Ethic" when introducing an edition of Audubon's *Birds of America* in 1981, Audubon was a man who "seemed obsessed with shooting." However, the Petersons say, "Audubon's real contribution was not the conservation ethic but awareness. That in itself is enough; awareness inevitably leads to concern."

Audubon was indeed aware and more than concerned about the "diminution of the forest." Farsighted in perceiving what others, particularly the farmers, were doing to the birds' resources, he was nearsighted when it came to his own excesses and those of his fellow shooters who killed far more birds than they needed to eat and, in Audubon's case, to draw.

In this century, when we finally started to run out of the unlimited plenty of green forests to cut down or tan prairies to plow under, a new technology — pesticides and fertilizers — together with vast quantities of water for irrigation, reinforced the idea of unlimited plenty by "doubling crop yields," according to the American Farmland Trust. The very cleared land which Audubon saw was smothered by a greater threat to wildlife.

The farms, a habitat far more hospitable to wild birds and animals and usually surrounded by woodlands, were covered over by shopping malls and new houses. "Since 1967," says Ralph Grossi, a third-generation dairy farmer and President of the Farmland Trust, "we've lost over twenty-five million acres of farmland — an area larger than the entire states of New Hampshire, Vermont, Massachusetts, Connecticut and New Jersey — to urban sprawl. Two-thirds of the new houses built between 1940 and 1990 "were outside cities on some of the country's best farmland," a condition which in Audubon's day would no doubt have been unthinkable.

As Audubon grew older he began to weary of senseless slaughter of birds and their young. Six years after publication of *Birds of America* had begun and Audubon was assured of some financial security, he went with his son John to Labrador. Audubon was horrified at the wanton destruction of birds he encountered there. Of the Labrador people he writes: "These people gather all the eider down they can find; yet so inconsiderate are they that they kill every bird which comes their way." Calling them the "eggers of Labrador," he concludes that "the eggers themselves will be the first to repent the entire disappearance of the myriads of birds that made the coast of Labrador their summer residences."

An older Audubon in Labrador could now see clearly what he had not perceived in those early icebound days on the Mississippi. Even without the planetary mapping by satellites which we have now enabling us to see the forests shrinking around that worldwide green belt once existing between the Tropic of Cancer and the Tropic of Capricorn, Audubon saw at last a clear pattern of extinction in destruction of habitat.

Only by mid-twentieth century did a naturalist find the conscience to speak out in what he called the need for a "land ethic." Like Audubon, Aldo Leopold began his love of animals as a hunter and lived to be a conservationist of a stature to be ranked with John Muir and Rachel Carson.

As early as 1936, speaking of the "new profession of wildlife management," Leopold pointed to threatened species, among them the migratory birds such as "the Trumpeter Swans, Curlews, and Sandhill Cranes." Furthermore, he recognized the "invisible interdependencies in the biotic community." And, like Audubon, he made a connection with the disappearance of habitat as the most destructive element in the continued existence of all life (Leopold, *The River of the Mother of God*).

Leopold saw how an age's attitude may limit its vision so that ethical attitudes extend to some form of life while ignoring the rights of other forms. He used Homer's story of the wandering Greek hero, Odysseus, as a model to illustrate his point. Much of the story hinges on the ownership of property, for when Odysseus returns home after his wanderings, he finds his kingdom overrun with suitors vying for the hand of his wife and for her property. His anger turns on the slave girls whom he suspects of misbehavior in his absence, and he hangs them. As Leopold says, "the ethical structure of that day covered wives, but had not yet extended to human chattels," the slave girls (Leopold, *A Sand County Almanac*).

Leopold dramatized a need for a new ethic "dealing with man's relation to the land and to the animals and plants which grow upon it. Land, like Odysseus' slave girls, is still property."

Toward the latter part of the nineteenth century, the realization was beginning to dawn in the minds of some Americans that the once abundant wildlife and endless wilderness were disappearing. Conservationist George Bird Grinnell, born in 1849 and a childhood student of Audubon's wife Lucy, grew up to be a Yale scientist who cherished the land. His deep respect for wildlife and wilderness was influenced by those Native American tribes, the Pawnee, the Cheyenne, and the Blackfeet, with whom he came into contact on his scientific expeditions in the unmapped West seeking paleontological specimens. A "bone hunter," or osteologist such as Grinnell understood the disappearance of a species. Not only was he witnessing the disappearance of wildlife, but he saw a way of human life vanishing. His travels brought him to respect those Native American tribes from whom he learned much about cherishing animals and land.

Grinnell lived a good long life as a naturalist and an editor, and he was an early ethnologist as well. He recorded his life among the various tribes of Plains

peak to the earth, and it will teach you.

Book of Job

Indians, whose ways of respect for animals and land were also disappearing.

In *Pawnee Hero Stories and Folktales*, he observes the Pawnees preparing for a buffalo hunt, and he anticipates Aldo Leopold's concept of "land ethic" by some fifty years when he writes of the Pawnees by his time confined to a reservation and "allowed" by the U.S. government to go on an annual buffalo hunt: "Now for a time, it was as it had been before the cornfields of the white man had begun to dot the river bottoms, before the sound of his rifle had made wild their game, before the locomotive's whistle had shrieked through the still, hot summer air."

Grinnell, respected as an early anthropologist, accomplished much in his life. Of all his many accomplishments, however, Grinnell might be most remembered as a founder of the Audubon Society — depending on your source. Grinnell was, if not the true founder of the Audubon Society, most admittedly the one who set in motion the idea of its founding. From his editorship at *Field and Forest*, he launched what the present National Audubon Society's biographer Frank Graham, Jr. calls "a society on paper." Grinnell's publication was called *Audubon Magazine*, established for the "protection of birds."

Eight years after Grinnell's magazine closed, Harriet (Mrs. Augustus) Hemenway of Boston called together some of her friends from the Boston Blue Book and distinguished naturalists such as Charles S. Minot, President of the American Society of Naturalists. This meeting in Harriet Hemenway's home resulted in the establishment of the Massachusetts Audubon Society, with Minot the first president.

John James Audubon's name was the most appropriate for the society, founded for the "protection of birds, especially the protection of the American Egret." As Frank Graham, Jr. says, "Audubon's idea of a bird, of birdness itself, passed into the nation's consciousness, and . . . influenced the way Americans looked at the natural world." Today's National Audubon Society has over five hundred chapters, and the *Audubon Magazine*, "speaking for nature," covers a broad spectrum of environmental issues in its pages.

Today, over 550,000 birders of the Audubon Society set out, armed not with guns but with field glasses and spotting scopes. They will encounter such species as the Great American Egret, its silhouette an Audubon Society logo.

This miraculous bird might have been totally extirpated for its glamorous breeding plumes, a commercial crop gathered for feather boas, had it not been for the work of the Audubon Society, who, like many others, began with defending one species and broadened to become environmentalists defending the planet.

The birdwatchers may walk beneath living oak trees upon which the Passenger Pigeon once perched, but they will see none. Nor will they focus their scopes on flocks of wild Trumpeter Swans wintering in Kentucky as Audubon did. They will have to go to the Yellowstone area or to Alaska for a glimpse of the Trumpeter — those "modern miracles" whom scientists once thought had disappeared, and, then when found, expected never to migrate across the United States again. Or, if they are really lucky, as Russell and I were, they will catch sight of the Trumpeters as they alight on a pond to which they have migrated, hundreds and hundreds of miles away from their summer breeding grounds in Minnesota.

D ESTROYER AND PRESERVER: HOMO SAPIENS

Few sportsmen have ever tried the sport of

learning something about the game they pursue...Why is this species

here? Whence does it come, where go?

THE ANCIENT HUNTER AND THE "NEW MIND"

The Ancient Hunter and the "New Mind"

In the last decade of the twentieth century, the 4000-year-old body of a man frozen in glacial ice is discovered in the Alps. His body, preserved upon the frozen heights, bears strange symbols; crosses and circles color his skin, mysterious ritualized tattoos put there perhaps to help and to protect him as he stalks his prey. He is clothed in animal hide, and he has with him a knife, a hatchet and a leather quiver filled with arrows.

Why did this man scale the mountain that long ago day four millennia before? Probably he was a hunter stalking game. The announcement of the mountain hunter's discovery in today's newspaper appears to be one of those accidental connections which seem to form patterns from events which are apparently random. For, just a few inches down from the announcement of the ancient mummy's find is the report of the opening of hunting season.

Outside of their common humanness, what possible connection could the ancient corpse have with the living body of a modern man? When alive the mountain man was no doubt propelled by many of the forces which yet propel the modern hunter. The same energy which drove that primal man up the mountain, possibly in search of game, will surge through the bodies of today's hunters on the opening of the season. In the United States, one of the animals they will be allowed to hunt legally is the Tundra Swan.

The ancient man's physical reactions, the excitement of the chase, the flow of adrenaline to give him a rush of energy for fighting or fleeing from the attacking game is alive in every cell of the hunter with a gun. When the modern hunter climbs into his four-wheel drive truck and turns the key, the old hunter's dynamism will be present in his body. He is living adumbration of that ancient mountain man. His physical reaction to the animals he pursues until the kill is with him yet.

SWANS OF THE WORLD

But our modern hunter faces an important difference as he heads his car or truck to the marshland. The power of the hunter over the animals has changed dramatically within the last 200 years.

This change has not occurred because of enhanced physical prowess evolving over the centuries. The mountain man was possibly stronger, his senses keener, but the modern hunter's technology has given him the edge which his body could not give him. "He can kill animals," in the words of theologian Elizabeth Dodson Gray, "faster than they can kill him." Therefore, the law-abiding modern hunter waits for the season to open, and he must hunt under laws and regulations agreed upon by his own species so that there will continue to be waterfowl or elk or trout for him to pursue in years to come.

The first hunters, of course, had no need of controls or management. In fact, just the opposite was true. The movement of wildlife controlled the hunter. Where the animals went, he followed, moving from place to place, a nomad. As he hunted prey, he was alert for the competition, the other preda-

n the very earliest time

when both people and animals lived on

earth

a person could become an animal if he

wanted to

and an animal could become a human

being.

Sometimes they were people

and sometimes animals

and there was no difference.

All spoke the same language.

"Magic Words"
An anonymous Eskimo poem
in *Shaking the Pumpkin;
Traditional Poetry of the Indian
North Americas*, ed. by
Jerome Rothenberg

Modern Inuit sculpture by
Nahstahpoka

tors, animals faster and more deadly than he. The migratory swans might appear like sudden gifts, some of them providing ready food, the rest disappearing into sky-places he could not follow.

Early civilization was tremendously outnumbered by animals. *Homo sapiens* was a small insignificant species, not only outnumbered, but totally unspecialized in abilities. An "amateur biologically of the animal kingdom," biologist Renée Dubos calls him. Not as strong or as fast or as camouflaged as the game he pursued, the hunter walking on two feet had to learn to make and to use weapons. He had to clothe himself in animal hide so that he could have a fighting chance to survive.

So overwhelmed by the forces of nature — raging storms or the animals lurking in the fearful night — *Homo sapiens* took a step forward into a new mind. Suddenly, as anthropologists perceive this being, he began to decorate himself with colored tattoos, wearing jewelry and painting the likeness of the animals he pursued such as bison or deer which came alive again on the walls of the cave. And he chose to depict himself as half-man, half-bird, the image of his spirit and of the power of flight which only his gods had. He began, as well, to live in groups which were the beginnings of social organization and which became, through cultivation of plants and gathering of harvests, a fixed rather than a totally errant way of life.

To define the changed being who began to emerge into civilized life, anthropologists dubbed the new creature *Homo sapiens sapiens*, or to use Jonathan Weiner's translation of the Latin, "man the doubly wise," an interesting irony of our own taxonomy.

Over a long period of time (when time is measured in human time) this "wise" creature spread out across the planet. Because he was not as specialized as the animals, he invented ways to live in the harsh environments he encountered. (The ancient mountain man stuck hay inside the hide boot to buffer the cold.) He began to use fire to keep himself warm inside his cave and to wear the fur and skins of animals to save him from freezing. For this blessing he thanked the animals, propitiating them or their spirits with chants and offerings. Rituals became, according to some scholars, the hunter's initiation ceremonies of the young. The myth of the hunter came alive. The "Lord of the

Animals" was born.

Some of the species passed over the landbridge from Siberia and spread out from the west of the continent of North America. One particular culture of the frozen Arctic northland, the Dorset people, were ancient hunters who became extinct by the time Columbus set out on his voyage of discovery.

Without the technology of the dogsled which the later people, the Eskimos, had, the Dorset did not survive. In his poem, "Lament for the Dorsets," Canadian poet Al Purdy imagines their lives. An old hunter carves the image of a swan from ivory. The poet gives the old man a face and a name, Kudluk. He is carving a two-inch ivory swan for a dead granddaughter:

> The carving is laid aside
> in beginning darkness
> at the end of hunger
> after a white wind
> blows down the tent, and snow
> begins to cover him
> After 600 years
> the long ivory thought
> is still warm.

Al Purdy

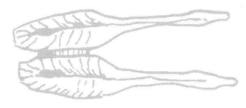

Ivory double swans, Dorset culture.

The hunters who came after the Dorset and replaced them were the Eskimos, or as they prefer to call themselves the Inuit, meaning simply "the people." These new peoples could move swiftly from place to place, skimming over ice and snow by using the dog sled to follow the animals they hunted. With their "long ivory thoughts still warm" they survived as hunters into the twentieth century. Due to the impossible conditions for agriculture—winters of snow and ice, summers of the morass of watery tundra, they were predominantly subsistence hunters rather than hunters and farmers as some early Native Americans became. Hunting, therefore, has been and still is, to some extent, their way of life. These hunters pursued the swan with simple but ingenious weapons requiring strength and skill. An early nineteenth-century explorer writes:

The Ugly Duckling
Hans Christian Andersen

> The multitudes of swans, ducks and geese resorting to the northern coast to breed, likewise aid in supplying the Esquimaux with food during their short but busy summer of two months. For their destruction a very ingenious instrument has been invented. Six or eight balls made of walrus-tooth and pierced in the middle are separately attached to as many thongs of animal sinew, which are tied together at the opposite end. When cast into the air, the diverging balls describe circles — like the spokes of a wheel — and woe to the unfortunate birds that come within their reach.

Quoted from Sir John Richardson's report
The Polar and Tropical Worlds, by G. Hartwig, 1877

Another method, from a late nineteenth-century report made by a Dr. Nelson and quoted by A. C. Bent, describes the Eskimos as hunting during the season the swans molt by spearing the swans from "their canoes or kayaks. Although unable to fly, it is not an easy task single-handed to capture them alive. The young men among the Eskimo consider it a remarkable exhibition of fleetness and endurance for one of their number to capture a bird by running it down." Fleet and strong, the Inuit lived in comparative isolation, visited by an occasional explorer or whaling ship, moving about in small groups pursuing the animals and worshipping them for the subsistence which they gave. The people and the animals were one. When they ate their prey the prey came alive within them. "A person could become an animal if he wanted to and an animal could become a human being." In this metamorphosis existed the spirit of the gods.

Thus hunting since earliest time has been a mystical experience for human beings, a basis for the spirit and life of a people. Robert Bly points to stories which exist throughout the world when the myth and folklore of the hunt began in "time before time." It is in these stories that the "Lord of Animals or Releaser of Animals crossed the line from the animals' side of things to the human side and back." And these stories suggest, says Bly, "a compact was made some time in the past between the human realm and the animal realm, and that agreement seems to be a tough one, providing obligations and rights on both sides" (Bly).

Like earliest man, the Inuit pursued and worshipped the animals they hunted, but they always gave back their veneration in the form of ritual and art. Their land lay more or less untouched, their fragile environment still pristine unlike the farmlands which lay to the south. But the dweller of cities finally found a use for their land. The north slope of Alaska was discovered to hold rich reserves of oil. Modern man's thirst for speed and headlong consumption of earth's resources demanded intrusion on the land of the Aleut, the natives of the far west of arctic North America, a people who share linguistic and cultural roots with the Inuit. One single disaster would decimate the Aleut hunter's way of life more quickly than the slaughter of the buffalo erased the spirit of the Plains tribes to the south. The Aleut of the late 1980s and early 1990s found themselves employed in a new hunt, a hunt not for food, but to fulfill their contract with the animals.

After the oil spill of the Exxon Valdez tanker, nearly eleven million gallons of oil floated into the waters and washed up on the shores of Alaska. The Aleut were employed as volunteers or paid workers to hunt the dying swans, geese, ducks, and other birds or mammals who foundered in the morass of petroleum. This hunt did not demand the incredible physical prowess of the ancient hunter, but it was a hunt nevertheless for survival: a survival of a way of life. The depredation of birds alone was extremely acute. As Dr. Calvin Lensink says of the thousands of birds lost, "The loss of birds is substantially higher than any other spill we know about anywhere in time."

Petroleum floating on water is particularly destructive to birds because the very system of natural oils from the preen gland is defeated. S. Dillon Ripley, Secretary Emeritus of the Smithsonian, pointed to

Tundra decoy used by modern hunters. Native Americans began custom of decoy carvings to lure birds. Head and neck, wood. Body canvas on wire this problem almost fifty years ago in World War II when he hunted the Eider Duck to save them when they were trapped in the oil spilled from bilges of tankers off the coast of New England.

Part of the birds' vulnerability, says Art Davidson in his account *In the Wake of the Exxon Valdez*, is that the "insulating layer of down feathers next to a bird's skin is protected by an interconnecting network of outer feathers that lock out water. If the outer feathers become oiled, they mat together, allowing water to leak through to the down, which then loses its ability to keep the bird warm." When the birds were found soaked with oil they were brought in for cleansing. But workers found another problem. As veterinarian Jessica Porter, one of the team of scientists working frantically to save the birds' lives, said, "If you don't get all the soap out, you may have a very clean bird, but one that can't float." But many times when the petroleum was washed away the natural oils of the birds were washed away also.

What the oil spill did to the sea and the bird life of Alaska, it did to the spirit of the Aleut. Even after the cleanup it was reported that people feared eating the birds, fish, and shell fish. "There's uncertainty," said one Native American, "of what the future will bring."

The immediate future has not brought much surcease to the Amerindian Tribes and Aleut who live in Alaska. Their religious ways, the very energy of the people, have been decimated like the wildlife around them. "What the white man does for sport and recreation and money," says the Chief of the Port Graham Alaska People, "we do for the life of our bodies, the life of our spirit."

The Alaska native peoples woke up one morning to look upon a changed world. Their way of life, the long chain of days reaching back to their most ancient times, their mythic beginnings, severed by one disaster. They stared at a shore littered with the sickening and dying animals of their spirit lives; the swift fish belly-up, the seal's fur clotted with oil, and the white feathers of the swan covered with black goo. It was a twilight of their gods, the beginning of a dark endless night of their souls.

As we presently know, a slow cumulative disaster has been building silently, unnoticed by many of us because our eyes are focused on the immediate threats. Evidence has been so fragmented as to escape our awareness. The transformation, like the overnight and obvious change of the Aleuts' world, has been so subtle and far flung that we never, until now, focused our sight upon it, turned our heads to listen to what was happening against a background noise barely imperceptible, what novelist Don Delilo calls "white noise."

In the early nineteenth century, Audubon wondered only mildly why the Trumpeter Swan, one of his beloved birds, had disappeared from the East Coast. Gradually, he did begin to perceive that the saw blade, the clear-cutting of trees and the ever-widening tillage of fields was taking the birds' habitat away from them. The canebrake of Kentucky was disappearing. These were fragmented bits of evidence that the world was changing. But his observations made little impression on the general public. Only now, after the disappearance of many species, has it dawned upon us that their loss and the loss of their habitat are endangering the welfare of our own species as well.

But our responses continue to be to the immediate, just as our ancient ancestor's responses were. The problem, say Robert Orstein and Paul Ehrlich, is that we react to crisis with our hunter's brain, a brain, according to neuroanatomist Paul McLean, which is only the first layer of a three-layered "paleopsychic process." This process is a historical accumulation of one layer (one brain) upon another. First, and the last to evolve, is the higher "thinking" brain, the brain involved with complex thought. Second is the limbic brain, the layer harboring our ancient emotional responses, "our human nature." Third is the reptilian or "crocodile" brain as Carl Sagan calls it. Coordinated within this layer are behaviors such as "territoriality, ritual encounters, greeting, courtship, formation of social hierarchies, migration and hoarding." Furthermore, this earliest brain harbors the "irresistible drives, impulses and compulsive behavior," including fighting, mating, and hunting (McLean quoted by Applewhite, *Paradise Mislaid*).

If you accept McLean's model of the brain, you will see how deeply hunting goes within the being of *Homo sapiens*. Some, such as mythologist Joseph Campbell, will connect the ceremony of hunting with early religious feelings, and allow that the impulses of hunting and the spirit (religious sense) are inextricably tied together within our ancient selves. Thus as a living being we

O silver throated Swan

Struck, struck! A golden dart

Clean through thy breast has gone

Home to thy heart.

Trill, trill, O silver throat!

O silver trumpet pour

Love for defiance back

On him who smote!

Down thy last living reach

Of river, sail the golden light—

Enter the sun's heart—even teach,

O wondrous-gifted Pain, teach thou

The god to love, let him learn how.

"The Dying Swan",
Sturge Moore

carry the genetic memory of ritual and hunt within us. It is no wonder, then, that a twentieth-century waterfowl artist/hunter might say, "You won't believe this, but hunting gives me a religious feeling," or that Osage writer John Joseph Matthews might describe feeling "like a god" after a hunt.

Our physical responses are immediate, just as our ancestors' reactions were to a bear's shadow cast across the mouth of a cave. We react to an automobile swerving headlong toward us in the same physiological manner, our bodies galvanized to meet the challenge or to flee it. Yet, say Ehrlich and Ornstein, because our hunter's mind may grasp immediate danger and our hunter's body react in preparing us to meet it, we are slow to perceive the gradual danger to the earth which has taken generations to bring about. This process speeded up in the last 200 years of the Industrial Revolution when we began to think of ourselves as beings apart from nature and to regard nature as something ticking along like a machine. Nature was "out there," the compact with the animals forgotten as we walked over the threshold of house or factory.

Unlike the rest of us, the Aleut saw a quick and disastrous change in their way of life brought about through the failure of technology. Another group of Eskimo, the Avilikmuit of Hudson's Bay, however, experienced a change through a technology they acquired and over which they indeed had some control. Ehrlich and Ornstein point to the experience of the Avilikmuit, an example of a primal culture still uniting the spiritual and the hunt, who were suddenly empowered with new technologies. Their rapid depletion of the very seals upon which they subsisted could be looked upon as a rapid parallel to our last 200 years, a fast-forward of the period from the dawn of the Industrial Revolution until now.

In 1952, say Ehrlich and Ornstein, the Avilikmuit Eskimo tribe, with a sudden windfall gained from the sale of white fox pelts, bought motorized fishing boats from Scotland and high-powered rifles with which to hunt. They took "pot shots" at the seal from the decks of their new boats:

> Unfortunately, much of the seal-hunting was done in the spring, when a layer of fresh water floated atop the salt water. Approximately twenty seals killed by rifle fire would sink out of reach in the fresh water for every one retrieved. With the old method of hunting using a harpoon equipped with a line affixed to a detachable point, virtually all animals killed had been recovered. As the intensity of the Eskimos hunting on the seals increased many-fold, the Avilikmuit still did not connect the growing scarcity of the animals with their own activities — because they believed the spirits controlled the supply of game (Ehrlich and Ornstein, 1989).

We are able to see in this account of the Avilikmuit, a clear portrayal of our ancient minds, minds still tied to the spirit of the hunt. However, with a second glance at the Eskimo story, we may also see our modern predicament in a nutshell. With our short-term brains and reflexes, we have filtered out the background dangers such as species depletion caused by our own technologies. We still have those short quick reflexes to danger, those reflexes which have enabled us to survive as a species until now. But we literally cannot perceive, or at least agree upon, the effects of gradual planetary changes. Our hunter's brains have not prepared us to do so.

We can see the threat of a rifle pointed at us in the same way our ancestor could see and react to a spear leveled at his throat, a claw flashing in moonlight, but those are not "threats generated by complex technological devices accumulated over decades by unknown people half a world away. Those are not threats such as the slow atmospheric buildup of carbon dioxide from auto exhaust, power plants, and deforestation."

We need, Ehrlich and Ornstein conclude, to replace our old minds with new ones. We need a "new" brain, as radically and culturally new as *Homo sapiens'* transition to *Homo sapiens sapiens*, hunter, agriculturist, artist.

Furthermore, the two scientists insist, the change needed is not a technological change — those great breakthroughs we all hope and pray science will accomplish: a cure for AIDS, a halt in the buildup of carbon dioxide. We need rather a cultural and perceptual change. We need to change "how we view the world and how we act on the discoveries we make." In other words, we need to develop "slow brains," ones which will comprehend the long process over many generations of past and future actions to our technological discoveries and our way of life.

It is certainly true that "cultural lag" is always with us. Ideas passing into society are slow to be put into action, just as the opposite is true of our physical reactions which are faster and triggered more quickly. However, the world and the envelope of thought which encircles it in the minds of collective humanity has always had its visionaries whose ideas are ahead of their time and their culture. Paul Ehrlich himself, co-author with Ornstein of the "new world, new mind" theory discussed above, noticed during his boyhood in the suburbs of New York that housing developments were taking over the landscape and as a result the butterflies were disappearing. Thus for thirty years, says John Nielsen, Ehrlich "studied the boom-bust cycles of the butterfly and worked on nontoxic ways to control pests." From his early observations of insect depletion,

Ehrlich came to the conclusion for which he is most known, the population bomb: the spread of *Homo sapiens sapiens* over the earth was, according to Ehrlich and many other biologists, a deadly threat to our own species.

There have been others who are endowed with a "new mind," the kind of mind which perceived long ago the danger to waterfowl and their habitat—this planet. Species of waterfowl have survived into this century because of the hard work of those with foresight enough to work towards saving many species.

There can be no doubt that a new awareness is dawning in the minds of people all over the globe at this very time: the end of the millennium. In the early nineteenth century, Audubon at last saw the danger. It took the society founded in his name, the Audubon Society, and the American Ornithologists' Union to fight for government legislation to stop commercial hunting and manage sport hunting so that waterfowl would be looked upon as life that must be preserved.

It has taken sport hunters as well, such as members of Ducks Unlimited, organized in Canada and the United States in the late 1930s for the "purpose of perpetuating and increasing waterfowl by preserving and protecting their breeding habitat." An insightful beginning, yet an argument rages over sport hunting. Some feel that it is a disgrace; others imbued with that age-old spirit of the hunt, feel it is a right. Attitudes on both sides are changing, however, and thus far one solution is to manage hunting. There can be no doubt that solving the problem of man and what Stephen Jay Gould calls man's "neighbor species" will take a "new mind." Others perhaps already endowed with a "new mind" have for years chosen to leave the argument behind and get on with their work.

Many individuals, sometimes those working alone or at least beginning their work alone, endeavor privately, then later publicly, to pursue the rearing of waterfowl. For example, S. Dillon Ripley, who would one day become head of the Smithsonian Institution, as a young man put in a pond at his home in Litchfield, Connecticut. The young man's project grew so that Ripley became a life-long aviculturist, breeding rare waterfowl, working within an international network of conservationists so that such species as the White-winged

Wood Duck, the Nene Goose and the Trumpeter Swan would still be part of the "veil of birds around the earth."

PRESERVING THE MAGIC HOUR

Russell and I stand in a hide, peering out at the Fenland before us, a watery marshland of Welney in East Anglia. November in these latitudes of England, dark falls rapidly, so rapidly that our eyes seem to be hooded by darkness. Only a faint trace of red and pink illumines the sky over the Ouse Wash. At 3:25 p.m., it is already past the soft light cherished by the photographer — the magic hour which comes only at twilight or dawn. My camera whirrs and clicks, the slow shutter laboring as if making a mighty effort to seize an image from the last light.

Where the camera's mechanism fails me, my eyes succeed in detecting movement. Hundreds of swans fly against the deep and final illumination of the horizon. In line after slanting line they drop down, and with a skid, splash silver clouds of water from the path of their trajectory. A "Swanfall" the English call this magnificent sight.

Five minutes later, the lights of Welney Wildfowl and Wetlands Centre come on, and the Wardens begin to wheel their barrows loaded with barley, wheat, and potatoes along the marshy edge below us. Now we can see the swans clearly. Directly below us in a white dazzle resident Mutes are feeding. At the perimeter of the floodlights' rays, flying down from darkness into light as if they were spontaneous matter released from the deep clouds, are wild Whoopers and Bewick's, mostly family groups, white-feathered parents with gray-feathered young. The high-flying Whoopers, sometimes climbing upward and leveling off at near stratospheric levels, have flown here to England from Iceland, and the Bewick's have come from their nesting grounds in Russia.

They will all winter here in the Fenlands of Anglia, their number growing from this evening's 1,000 swans to 5,000 wild swans. Each morning and evening they will be fed as the days shorten toward the solstice, then gradually lengthen until in early spring the urge to migrate will trigger their flight. Northward they'll fly in early spring, their bodies geared with energy to sustain them for the 2,500-mile flight to their high Arctic nesting grounds.

As the last one to leave the "hide" (a term which in American English is a duck "blind") I walk back in the immense darkness along a walkway toward the Welney Wildlife and Wetlands Trust Centre buildings, one of the nine trust centers founded by Sir Peter Scott. The film inside my camera will later yield only blackness, but the sight of those wild swans stays with me, illumined at the back of my brain.

A sunrise, another magic hour, this time in the far west of England all the way across the Island from Welney. Here at Slimbridge Wildfowl and Wetlands Trust Centre, I have photographed White-winged Wood Ducks, luckily in daylight, for these "rarest ducks in the world" take to the shadows, preferring shade like the deep forests of their Asian homelands. I have sketched an aging Jankowski's Swan, so slightly different from the Bewick's — the yellow prong on the Bewick's bill is not as pronounced as this old fellow's, and over the eye is slightly more yellow coloration. I have gazed at Black-necked Swans, Black Swans, and a young Coscoroba still slightly dappled.

As I walk along the path of the Wildfowl Centre, I see the willow stakes. These gray weatherworn stakes of lumber are used as fencing, but to Sir Peter Scott they were metaphors of life beginning again. The miraculous sprouting of "dead" lumber was one of the gestures of nature Scott seemed most to enjoy. After walkways or special areas were fenced off with pickets made from the willow wood, which were sunk in the marshy earth, the stakes sprouted, leafing out like young trees.

Sir Peter Scott is not here now. The sculpture of him by Jacqueline Shakleton at the entrance to Slimbridge bears only the date 1946 when he founded the Trust. He died just before his eightieth birthday on August 29, 1989, but his remarkable vision in the creation of wildfowl and wetlands centers and his paintings of wildfowl survive, greening like the willow stakes.

Wild geese and, as I was afterwards to learn their close relatives the swans, are very special birds because their society is based on a permanent pair bond and a family life which keep the young with their parents until breeding time comes round again. It took me a little time after I had learned these things before I decided to give up all shooting. I have not fired a gun for thirty-two years.

Peter Scott
Observations of Wildlife

Sculpture of Sir Peter Scott at the entrance to Slimbridge.

With a foreknowledge that he and his fellow explorers would perish in the blizzards of Antarctica before reaching the South Pole, Robert Falcon Scott wrote his last messages to his "widow," his wife Kathleen, an accomplished sculptor and mother of his son Peter. "I know," wrote Captain Scott, "you will keep him in the open air."

The boy, Peter Markham Scott, then aged two-and-a-half, spent much of the rest of his life in the open. And his effort and energy, particularly as an early environmentalist since the 1930s when he began his work to conserve waterfowl on a worldwide basis, has enabled many of us, including Russell and me, to get out into the open to see and to observe waterfowl.

The life of this remarkable man was one of dedication. He was so multitalented that a longtime friend and fellow naturalist Gerald Durrell wrote of him, "There is only one way to describe Peter and that is to say that he is a magical man with skills that would have made Merlin envious."

Had it only been for his accomplishments as a sportsman — winning a Bronze Medal in Olympic yachting, a first place for the Prince of Wales Cup and a second for America's Cup, the accomplishments of a son of a famous explorer and artist mother would have been enough. In addition to his yachting prowess and victories, he became British Gliding Champion in 1963.

However, when asked just before age eighty the accomplishments of which he was most proud, he listed first his many paintings of wildfowl, his creation of the Wildfowl and Wetlands Trust, and his eighteen books covering a wide variety of natural history. These included *The Swans* in which he and members of the Wildfowl and Wetlands Trust such as Andrew Dawnay, Myrfyn Owen, and Janet Kear ranged over a number of topics compiling the scientific and cultural lore of one of their favorite genus of bird.

Near Slimbridge's Yuen-Peng McNeice Observatory, which overlooks Sir Peter's and his wife Lady Philippa's house and the marshlands of the Severn River, at least twenty-five Nene Geese, those handsome waterfowl indigenous to the islands of Hawaii, strut toward me in a startling and loose gaggle. They are birds filled with curiosity and friendliness, unlike some of their relatives who have been used traditionally as sentinels. I offer a Nene grain from my hand and it takes it with the gentle care and fastidiousness of a truly sociable

Sir Peter Scott's observation tower at Slimbridge.

bird. Perhaps this very goose has been hand-fed by Peter Scott. Here poised to eat are half the entire population of Nene geese who once existed in the wild; in 1961, there were only fifty Nene alive.

There might not be any Nene Geese anywhere in the world if Peter Scott and the Wildfowl Trust had not labored so diligently to rear them thousands of miles away from their home in the Pacific. Furthermore, the Bewick's Swans and the Whoopers have found safe refuge in England because of him. Until he enticed a Bewick's to land at Slimbridge, there had only been scattered reports of Bewick's in Ireland and the English fenland and Whoopers wintering in the north, particularly Scotland. They had, however, never wintered over in such great numbers as they have in recent years at Slimbridge, Welney, or other places of the Wildfowl Trust.

In Peng Observatory, I look out to see the wild Bewick's Swans. On the walls of the observatory is a chart identifying each of the Bewick's with name and bill marking. This extraordinary study (spoken of earlier in the Bewick's Chapter) involving individual bill marking of the swans has enabled the Trust to undertake an incredibly detailed recording and research. On another wall is a typewritten notice that Scott's daughter (Dr. Dafila Scott) and Dr. Eileen Rees are going to the Pechora Delta of Russia "to determine the distribution of Slimbridge-ringed birds in their breeding area on the Delta 63."

In December 1990, sixty-three Bewick's Swans were caught at Slimbridge and marked with yellow dye on the tail and wing tips. At Martin Mere and other Wildfowl and Wetland Trust Centres, seventy-eight Bewick's Swans were caught and marked similarly with yellow dye. Although the swans will shed their yellow-dyed feathers during their summer molt, Dr. Scott and Dr. Rees are able to identify the Bewick's who have wintered at the Trust Centre not only by their plastic legrings, but by their black and yellow bill markings. Thus when looking through their field glasses at Bewick's Swans, Dr. Scott and Dr. Rees can do what no other scientists making a census of swans can do anywhere in the world thus far: they can identify an individual bird by its own appearance, the characteristic bill marking unique to the Bewick's. Thousands of miles from their home in England, Dr. Scott and Dr. Rees might raise their field glasses to their eyes and call each swan by name.

Sir Peter Scott feeding Nenes

173

They did indeed discover an old "familiar" in a vast area of the Russian delta where only recently have even citizens been allowed. Although 300 yards away, they caught sight of the Bewick's Swan Ieun (Welsh for Ian), which had first been catalogued in England in 1990. When they returned from the Pechora Delta, they caught sight of him in England the following fall (D. Scott).

Jet-lagged, I arrive home from England aboard a 747 wide-bodied jet. A 5000-mile trip airborne, just about the same distance a Bewick's Swan accomplishes on the wing round-trip to Slimbridge and back to the Pechora Delta of Russia. I'm ready to unpack my camera bag loaded with used film and notebooks full of field notes when the phone rings. It's Al, my game manager friend who let me know about the Minnesota Trumpeter family last spring. "There's a report of two wild Trumpeters," Al says.

"Where?" I ask sleepily. He gives me explicit directions. They are at a small lake just outside the city. It's Armistice Day, November 11, 1992.

Jet-lag or not, I pick up my camera and head for the car. Wild things don't wait. This might be my only chance to see them. As I head out the expressway, I realize that I haven't slept for over twenty-four hours.

I make a right, a left, then go through a stoplight. Finally the long, low building described in Al's directions appears. I turn again and cross a cattle guard. Then I see the glint of a little lake ahead.

There are two of them. Trumpeters. I twist my long-range lens into focus and I see the yellow collar with black numbers. It's 59-NC from Hennepin Parks with the mate of unknown origin. They've migrated here from Minnesota for at least the second year, and they have chosen a different lake from the one Russell and I saw them on earlier. There are no young ones with them this time.

The pair are feeding calmly among a flock of Gadwall Ducks, totally at home and completely unaware that, because they have survived at least two migrations over immense distance to the same area, they are no doubt among the living wonders of the western world.

THE GLORIOUS RESTORATION

The swans of the world have long been regarded by humans as one of the marvels of nature. Important and mysterious enough to appear in myth, folklore and legend worldwide wherever swans are found, they have been looked upon as a link to the celestial. With the enigmatic powers of gods, the migratory swans suddenly appeared from the sky, as gods did on earth for a time, then vanished like skygods into the heavens.

Of all the northern swans the most mysterious in its passage has been the Trumpeter. Venerated by the Amerindian — The Great White Swan of the Osages, the Red Swan of the Ojibway — it was reported by European colonizers as early as 1630. Yet still to this day, many of its comings and goings have been shrouded in mystery.

Before Winston E. Banko sat down at his desk to write his comprehensive work *The Trumpeter Swan*, he clearly researched every historical report he could find of Trumpeters since American Colonial days. Certainly by the late 1950s Banko knew more or at least as much as anyone alive at that time about the Trumpeter Swans. Though he knew of Trumpeters in Alaska, even he could not know the extent of the large yet uncensused populated nesting in Alaska. For (as cited earlier) the U.S. Fish and Wildlife Service pilots did not count the population of 1,124 swans in interior south coast Alaska until 1959, the same year Banko's work was put in print. Furthermore, it is not until fairly recently in the history of the Trumpeter that the USFWS made a more comprehensive count of the Alaska swans and discovered to everyone's surprise that not 1,000, but 2,487 Trumpeters inhabited Alaska and migrated south. These were migratory, not sedentary birds. The find was a mother lode of genetic material for aviculturists who wished to restore or to reintroduce the Trumpeter to the lower forty-eight states.

There was a time in this century when no one believed or even dared hope the Trumpeter Swan would ever return to its lost tradition of migrating across the lower forty-eight states. The swan had apparently lost the knowledge of migratory routes which adults pass on to their young. Most scientists believed that the Trumpeter had become a "sedentary" bird, one who nests, rears young and winters over essentially in the same place, but which is free to fly. In this case, the Trumpeter's permanent habitat was thought to be the Yellowstone area where it had withdrawn to escape mankind.

Furthermore, there was not a great optimism about the Trumpeter's chance of survival. In 1939, Peter Scott spoke of the Trumpeter as very close to "going the way of the Great Auk and the Passenger Pigeon." With words of deep concern, he wrote in *Wild Chorus*: "the largest of all waterfowl is only by the narrowest of margins still included in the Avifauna of the world."

Another European, also concerned with birds the world over, arrived in the United States shortly after Scott wrote of the Trumpeter. When French ornithologist and writer Jean Delacour came to America in the 1940s to escape World War II's invading armies and the final ravaging of his second private collection of rare birds (the first was destroyed in World War I), he came here, a French aristocrat, world renowned, world travelled, a seasoned observer and researcher of the world's avifauna. He brought with him only the money in his pocket he was allowed to take from war-torn France, and he started a new life. From the Old World tradition of private game parks or exotic private collections, he joined the New World's system of public National Parks and Wildlife Refuges: as part of his new life he became a consultant to the U.S. Fish and Wildlife Service, engaged to act upon "waterfowl problems in government preserves and particularly to help with the problems of the Trumpeter Swan." Thus he went to Red Rock Lakes, the refuge in Montana near the Yellowstone established to protect the Trumpeter and its habitat where, as he says, "the biggest population of these swans in the United States has survived" (*The Living Air*).

Delacour and other scientists of the United States and of the world were aware other Trumpeter populations existed in Alaska and Canada, but very little hard information existed concerning any migratory movement of those swans, although some flew from Canada to winter near the Yellowstone.

The problem as Delacour and others saw it, even some years later when he wrote his extensive and valuable taxonomy *Waterfowl of the World*, is that the Trumpeter known at Yellowstone, compared to its free-flying highly migratory relatives (Tundra, Whooper, and Bewick's) is a "fairly sedentary bird, much like the Mute, only wandering far enough to find open water and food. It breeds as far south as it can and winters as far north as possible while the Whooper, Whistler, Jankowski's, and Bewick's nest in the far north and accomplish long and regular journeys south to return punctually in the spring."

Clearly, and all seemed to agree on this, the Trumpeter's survival within the United States had been only because of its withdrawal to the comparative isolation of the Yellowstone area where warm springs and geothermal pools enabled it to nest and to care for its young and to winter over in the same territory without migrating over what Winston Banko describes as the "heavily gunned flyways of the United States."

After the swan was protected, first by the Migratory Bird Treaty and then by safeguarding its chosen and continuous habitat near Red Rock Lakes of the Yellowstone area, its numbers under the care of Winston Banko, manager of the refuge, grew from thirty-five cygnets and adults counted in 1931 to 488 adults and young in 1957.

But scientists such as Banko and Delacour knew the swan would eventually reach a plateau in its population growth at the Yellowstone. The time would come when the demands of the adults and young would be beyond the ability of the area to sustain them. The "carrying capacity," or resources of the land, would be overburdened by this "savage and jealous bird" as Delacour describes it when speaking of its territorial behavior demanding large areas in which to nest and bring up young.

The swans had to be moved to new areas which could sustain them. And the biologists were buttressed with the hope that the swans would learn to stay where they were translocated and to found new homes and swan dynasties.

The difficulty was — and still is — that new sites must be suitable for

spice bis senex laetantis agmine cycnos . . .

Behold! Twelve swans rejoicing in a long line.

Vergil
The Aeneid

177

swans, particularly sites must have open water all year, because the swans would not migrate and, said Delacour, "they often perish when ice fills up their rivers and open ponds."

Even with a massive effort to transfer the Trumpeters to refuges in Wyoming, Oregon, and Nevada, the Trumpeter population today is slender compared to the vast numbers which existed before the commercial hunters (such as those of the Hudson's Bay Company) sold a total of 17,671 swanskins between 1853 and 1877 — 2,000 more than are counted in the entire world 1980s population, (1980s population estimate: 15,000 Trumpeters).

The Yellowstone Trumpeters' population may sometimes be threatened as it was in the winter of 1988–1989, with the very peril Delacour had feared almost fifty years before: the winter freeze-up.

Ruth Shea (whom you saw earlier in the "Lifespan" section in the tragic winter of 1989), an Idaho Fish and Game Biologist who has devoted much research, work, and care to the Trumpeter, prophesied that "something would happen to the swan." Whether that something would be disease or a freeze-up, she didn't know, but she felt that the population was imminently threatened. And she was right. A bizarre freeze-up of the once-flowing warm waters and the food supply of the swans disappeared into the ice beyond the reach of even those powerful birds. Thus occurred, to Ruth Shea's dread, a full-blown worst case of her imagining in 1989 and again in 1990.

Even with humans making desperate attempts to feed the starving swans, Shea and the other naturalists watched helplessly as swans died in silence with no melodic swansong to herald their death.

With the resilience those who work with natural forces seem to find, and despite the terrible loss, Shea and other biologists of the U.S. Fish and Wildlife Service, state agencies, and private agencies began, according to Judy Mills in *National Wildlife* "an emergency trapping program to transport swans to food-rich open waters in Idaho, Utah, and Wyoming."

Capturing the long-necked swan is comparable to balancing on a tight rope while juggling ten apples in the air. The descriptions of the difficulty runs all through swan literature; Audubon's friend Dr. Sharpless described the task in detail. Wings and feet are the greatest threat. But when you get the wings held

When the swan must fix his eye

Upon a fading gleam,

Float out upon a long

Last reach of glittering stream

And there sing his last song.

The Tower
William Butler Yeats

178

down, the long neck with the powerful bill can curl around and give you a sharp, bruising bite, unless, of course, the swan goes into a kind of thanatosis, a death-feigning state which some animals achieve when captured by a predator. Thus the effort was a cold and dangerous one. Said Rod Parker of Idaho Fish and Game, "we had people fall into the river; their clothes froze as soon as they came out of the water."

Trumpeters still died in the storms of winter, but more survived. Shea and her colleagues say that if even a few of the relocated swans fly and return to the relocation areas, biologists will view the project as a success. The swans will have succeeded in the wild — an important principle behind the restoration of the Trumpeters, projects which now encompass Michigan under Joe Johnson and Wisconsin under Sumner Matteson, modeled on the program begun in Minnesota by Laurence Gillette when the eggs of the Red Rock Lake Trumpeters were incubated.

It is important to remember that these birds are reared to be released into the wild. They are brought up in captivity, and all sorts of elaborate precautions have been experimented with to keep the birds from becoming overly imprinted by humans. When the birds are sufficiently mature, around age two, then and only then are they released to fly freely and to find new homes. To survive under all the modern day threats of power lines, lead shot, and predators they must have what some call the spirit to "fly or die."

A good example of the spirit to fly rather than to die is the pair of wild swans Russell Studebaker and I first saw in the spring of 1991 and on their return the following fall. They landed in their second migration from Hennepin Parks, Minnesota, here in Oklahoma on a pond near Tulsa. It was in the fall, and they had no cygnet with them. Even with only two swans on it, the pond did not have sufficient food for them to survive long. They stayed from November 11, 1991, until a few days after Christmas. Before they left their city pond to inhabit another lake some ten miles away, they would fly away, leaving for an hour or so, cruising above factories and highways which crowded so near the pond.

Gradually they stayed away longer and longer. Finally they seemed to discover that the pond did not have enough food for them. Their new home was a food-rich lake, isolated and protected, the same lake which they had inhabited on their last migration. They left in the spring. The following winter, in what seemed to be a gift of the gods, we found them again. This time we had to drive 100 miles or so northward to that vast area which has long been the land of the Osage tribe who made the Great White Swan their bird of peace.

The day we found them was a twenty-degree January day, and the cold pond on which the swans floated seemed to be still as pewter. Scorched across the hill behind them was a great swath of black, a fall burn-off of bluestem grass. 59-NC, with his yellow and black Hennepin collar, and his mate edged along the far margin of the pond, leading their four dusky cygnets. They seemed wary of us, and we kept our distance outside the barbed wire fence.

Along the bumpy road beside the pond came a pickup truck. When it jolted to a halt, a woman and her two children, a boy and girl, got out and headed straight towards the pond, hesitating only long enough for the boy to hold the barbed wire in two arcs while his mother and sister stepped lightly through. The woman crouched beside the pond calling, "Co-oo-m-me on-n-n-n," to the swans in a voice sounding very like their own call. 59-NC tilted his head to the side, then circled towards the woman on the bank. The female brought up the rear, guarding the cygnets as they all responded to the woman. We were in the presence of one of those people who understand the way of birds, and this was her family's land and the land of their ancestors.

When the woman and her children turned to go back to their truck, the swan family began their mutual head-dipping signals. When she paused to greet us, for she obviously sensed we had come to see the swans, the swan family took off in a rush, slanting upward in a line, the two adults in the rear, the four cygnets flashing against the dark, scorched hill. They turned again, gaining altitude, then turned once more, heading straight over us, calling "ko-ho-o-o." It is this trait of circling back which has made the Trumpeter an easy "shining mark" for gunners of the past. But six of the world's largest waterfowl flying now in a straight line against the deep winter sky made a glorious sight.

The female was no longer of "unknown origin." We had spied a legband with the number 55-NC. She was a Hennepin Parks swan released to the wild in 1990. Perhaps it was just one of those lucky accidents of nature, but 59-NC and 55-NC had chosen a better place each visit here in Oklahoma. Now they had found a perfect place, hospitable for a large swan family to winter over. And they would come back again.

They stayed on the family's ranch of 10,000 acres, frequently moving from pond to pond, for they had eighty-seven to choose from. They appeared daily on the lake near the ranch house, calling to the family, becoming a part of their lives, until one day in early March, they left as suddenly as they had arrived. They returned, waking the woman and her family from sleep, circling above her house and announcing their presence the following fall.

Wary enough to make four successful migrations, to find all the routes south which had been lost to Trumpeters since they vanished from Minnesota over 100 years ago, 59-NC and 55-NC had become migratory birds again. Their skyborne kingdom restored, their ancient knowledge of migration routes newly found and passed on to their young; they are visible links to the best of human effort in restoring to nature some of what we once heedlessly took away.

Drawn once more to Swan Lake Park, I go to stand beside the fence, watching the resident Trumpeter pair. The male gazes at me, then returns to preening. A spring wind urges a tuft of down from his bill, and the white fluff migrates like a winged seed through the fence. Tumbling and turning, it spins along, a white fluff coded with genetic information. A microbiologist passing by might pick it up, take it to the laboratory, and tell you something of this creature, the thumbprint of its deep genetic mapping.

The body of knowledge accumulated by natural scientists ever since Aristotle appears, like nature, to be ever-changing. A new fact may very well put a new face on an older notion. As scientists explore the world deeper and farther, as they investigate life and its planetary environment, human concepts seem to molt, casting off one conception for another. Even with all the new technologies for research, part of the conceptual molt still depends on observations in the field. Birders or biologists find new readings of the code the biotic world sends out — some have the creativity to interpret them.

A part of that world as we are, we humans, even a few scientists, continue with preconceptions. Judgments formed by personal allegiances prevail when it comes to the natural world. Ideological warfare has been known to break out among those who prefer one species of swan over another. Species preferences are upheld as fiercely as a nesting swan defending its territory. Occasionally there are apparently valid reasons for these attitudes, such as overpopulation or underpopulation of a particular species, each condition in its own way a possible threat to the species' survival — and by extension to our own survival.

Swan biologists throughout the world, meeting in Oxford, England, in 1989, realized the need for worldwide collaboration to enhance their study of the swan. "Such collaboration," writes Susan L. Earnst in her *Synthesis of the Third International Swan Symposium*, "will make swans one of the few [classifications of birds] that will be studied across the breeding range of each species." Furthermore, "the migrant swans will be among the only long-distance migrants that can be studied throughout their annual cycle, despite migrations which take them across borders of nations."

The Trumpeter Swan beside the fence, hatched seven years ago from the egg of a Red Rock Lake female and an Alaska male, will never fly across borders of nations as many of his relatives in the wild may fly. But he is a messenger of the high kingdom of the skies for all the parkgoers who come to see him. For, even with the closeup view we may have of them as they float on park lakes and ponds, or with the distant glimpse we may catch of them in the remote wilds, the swans of the world remain mysterious presences to which human beings are constantly drawn.

Altricial   Birds which begin life mostly blind and featherless are altricial, the young birds are totally dependent on parent birds for food and care.

Anthropocentric   A human-centered point of view which interprets nature as either beneficial or detrimental to the human being.

Archaeopteryx lithographica   A Jurassic period fossil the size of a crow which was found in Germany. The fossil creature is the first found to have shown that it bore feathers and therefore was capable of flight.

Australian realm   A geographic realm which includes Australia, New Zealand, and New Guinea, it is one of six life-zones on the planet. Biogeographers distinguish the zones by distinctive lifeforms. The other five realms are: Nearctic (North America and part of Mexico), Palearctic (Europe, Asia north of the Himalayas, Afghanistan, Iran, and North Africa), Neotropical (South and Central America, part of Mexico, and the West Indies), Ethiopian (Africa south of the Sahara, Madagascar, and Arabia), Oriental (Asia south of the Himalayas, India, Sri Lanka, Malay Peninsula, southern China, Borneo, Sumatra, and the Philippines).

Binomial system   The system of classifying an organism with a two-word name: genus and species, e.g., *Cygnus* (Genus) *atratus* (Species) for Black Swan. The Arctic swans (because they are thought to be conspecific by some) have trinomial or three-word names.

Biosphere   The entire zone of air, land, and water existing on the surface of earth which supports life.

Biome   An easily distinguished large communal unit of diverse lifeforms.

Captive waterfowl   Ducks, geese, and swans who live in a partially domestic state because their flight feathers are clipped; thus, they cannot fly away.

Cloaca   Located in the bird's posterior area, the cloaca completes the bird's digestive tract; thus, it is the chamber which receives the feces and urogenital products.

Conspecific   Those organisms considered to belong to the same species, which have yet enough distinguishing features to allow for distinction: The Arctic swans (Whooper, Bewick's, Tundra, and Trumpeter) are considered by some authorities to be conspecific.

Decoy   1. In American-English: a three-dimensional likeness of a particular fowl which is used by hunters to lure wild birds, a practice begun by Native Americans. 2. In British-English: a large netting shaped like a cornucopia set in water into which waterfowl are lured when they mass together to form a single unit facing a predator. The waterfowl guarding against the predator follow it into the netting. In this case they follow a red dog chosen for its fox-like look.

Display   A ritualistic or formalized behavior which birds assume under peak life conditions such as mating or threat.

Domesticating birds   The process of isolating birds from their wild fellows and breeding them selectively, thus producing a genetically different specimen from their wild ancestors.

Endemic population   The population of birds native to a particular area or region.

Extirpation   The complete destruction or extermination of a species.

Extinct   A species which no longer has a living example.

Genotype   The DNA structure of an organism based on its hereditary or genetic factors.

Gondwanaland   A great southern hemisphere landmass which included Antarctica, South America, Africa, Madagascar, Australia, and New Zealand, which began to break up about 135 million years ago.

Ground-staring   A part of the posture in a bird's display characteristic of the four Arctic swans holding the wings extended from the sides of the body and extending the neck downward, pointing towards the ground.

Imprinting   The process of forming a strong attachment or bond to a parent or object which takes place shortly after precocial birds are hatched.

Mandible   The bird's lower bill, comparable to the human jaw: in modern birds it is toothless.

Nidiculous   Just-hatched birds incapable of leaving the nest and therefore needing much parental care.

Nidifugous   Literally, nest-fleeing birds. Used to describe just-hatched birds such as swan cygnets which are ready to leave the nest.

Pathetic fallacy   A literary critic's term for a characteristic of those writers who wrote of nature's plenty as existing only for man's use.

Phenotype   The physical appearance of an organism which is based on hereditary or genetic factors.

Precocial   Birds which may leave the nest after hatching and do not require the extreme feeding and care which altricial birds need.

Radiation (adaptive)   The movement of a species from its area of origin into a wider region.

Speciation   The slow process of change and adaptation through which a new species arises.

Species   A group or unit of organisms which interbreed and are reproductively separate from other groups of organisms.

Syrinx A physiological structure of birds located at the end of the trachea which produces sound by vibration of a membrane caused by a rush of air.

Taxonomy The principle of naming life forms and classifying them into categories beginning with the broad (Kingdom) down to the narrow classification (Species). An example of Swan classification and naming:

Kingdom: *Animalia* (animals)

Phylum: *Chordata* (vertebrates)

Class: *Aves* (birds)

Order: *Anseriformes* (swans, geese, ducks, and screamers)

Family: *Anatidae* (swans, geese, and ducks)

Genus: *Cygnus* (swans)

Species:
    coscoroba (not considered by all to be a true swan)

    olor (Mute)

    atratus (Black)

    melanocoryphus (Black-necked)

    cygnus (Whooper)

    Subspecies (considered by some):
        columbianus bewickii (Bewick's)

        columbianus jankowskii (Jankowski's or Eastern Bewick's)

        columbianus columbianus (Tundra)

        cygnus buccinator (Trumpeter)

Note: This is a very simplified version of the classifications. For finer distinctions, see Sir Peter Scott's *A Coloured Key to the Wildfowl of the World.*

Waterfowl The vernacular or common term (used in American-English) for the family of ducks, geese and swans classified as *anatidae.*

Wildfowl The vernacular or common term (used in British-English) for the family of ducks, geese and swans classified as *anatidae.* The I.W.W.A., founded by Jean Delacour, takes note of this distinction between the Americans and British by calling the association the International Wild Waterfowl Association.

Yellowstone population A short term used to designate the Trumpeter Swan population native to the area in and around Yellowstone National Park which includes areas in Montana, Idaho, and Wyoming. It is also called Rocky Mountain population.

Alexander, Hartley B.: *North American*, Vol. 1, *Mythology of All Races*, Archaeological Institute of America, 1928.

Allison, Sue and Simons, Carol: "A Snowdrift of Swans," *Life*, March 1988.

Andersen, Hans Christian: *The Complete Hans Christian Andersen Fairy Tales*, ed. Lily Owens, from editions published in 1883, 1889.

Anesaki, Masaharu: *Japan*, Vol. III, *Mythology of All Races*, Archaeological Institute of America, 1928.

AOU Checklist of North American Birds: American Ornithologists' Union, 1983.

Applewhite, E.J.: *Paradise Mislaid*, St. Martin's Press, 1991.

Aristophanes*:* "The Birds*,*" *The Complete Greek Drama*, Vol. 2, ed. Whitney J. Oates and Eugene O'Neill, Jr., Random House, 1938.

Armstrong, Edward A.: *Discovering Bird Courtship*, Shire Publications, 1978.

Armstrong, Edward A.: *The Life and Lore of Birds*, Crown Publications, 1980.

Audubon, John James: *The Birds of America*, Vol. VI, An unabridged replication of the work first published by J. J.

Audubon and J. B. Chevalier, 1840–44, Dover Publications, 1967.

Audubon Nature Encyclopedia, Vol. 10, sponsored by National Audubon Society, Curtis Publishing Co., 1965.

Audubon Reader. ed. Scott Russell Sanders, Indiana Univ. Press, 1986.

Audubon Society Field Guide to North American Birds, Borzoi Books, Alfred Knopf, 1988.

Banko, Winston: *The Trumpeter Swan*, Univ. of Nebraska Press, 1980.

Bellrose, Frank: *Ducks, Geese and Swans of North America*, Wildlife Management Inst., Stackpole Books, 1980.

Bent, Arthur Cleveland: *Life Histories of North American Birds* (originally published in 1925 as Smithsonian Institution National Museum Bulletin No. 130) Dover Publications, Inc., 1962.

Bly, Robert: *Iron John*, Addison-Wesley Publishing Co., 1990.

Boyd, Hugh, ed.: *The Wildfowl Trust, Seventeenth Annual Report*, 1964–65.

Brent, Peter: *Captain Scott*, Weidenfield and Nicolson, 1974.

Brooke, Michael and Birkhead, Tim, eds.: *The Cambridge Encyclopedia of Ornithology*, Cambridge University Press, 1991.

Bruchac, Joseph: "Creation," *Stone Giants and Flying Heads*, Crossing Press, 1979.

Bullfinch, Thomas: *The Age of Fable or Beauties of Mythology*, S.W. Tilton & Co., 1855.

Burnie, David: *Bird*, Alfred A. Knopf, 1988.

Burns, Louis F.: *Osage Indian Customs and Myths*, Ciga Press, 1984.

Butler, David and Don Merton: *The Black Robin*, Oxford University Press, 1992

Campbell, Bruce: " Bird Behavior," *Birds*, Hamlyn Publishing Group.

Campbell, Joseph: *The Masks of God*, Viking Press, 1968.

Cansdale, G.S.: *Animals and Man*, Hutchinson Publication, 1952.

Collins, Henry Hill, ed.: *Bent's Life Histories of North American Birds* Vol. I, Harper & Brothers, 1960.

Darwin, Charles: *The Origin of Species*, Mentor Edition, New American Library of World Literature, 1958.

Darwin, Charles: *The Voyage of the Beagle*, Heritage Press, 1957.

Davidson, Art: *In The Wake of the Exxon Valdez*, Sierra Club Books, 1990.

Delacour, Jean: *The Living Air: The Memoirs of an Ornithologist*, Country Life, 1966.

Delacour, Jean: *The Waterfowl of the World*, Vol. I, Country Life, 1973.

Dixon, Roland B.: *Oceanic*, Vol. IX in *Mythology of all Races*, Marshall Jones Company, 1916.

Dubos, Renee: *So Human an Animal*, Chas. Scribners, Sons, 1968.

Dunne, Pete: *The Feather Quest*, Dutton, 1992.

Durant, Mary and Michael Harwood: *On the Road with John James Audubon*, Dodd, Mead Quality Paperback, 1984.

Durrell, Gerald: *Two in the Bush*, Viking Press, 1966.

Ehrlich, Paul and Anne Ehrlich: *Extinction*, Random House, 1981.

Ehrlich, Paul and Robert Ornstein,: "New World, New Mind," *New Age Journal*, July/Aug. 1989.

Earnst, Susan L.: "The Third International Swan Symposium, A Synthesis," Proceedings of the Third International Swan Symposium,*Wildfowl*, Supplement No. 1, 1991.

Eiseley, Loren: *Darwin's Century*, Anchor Books, 1961.

Evans, Mary and Andrew Dawnay: "Swans in Mythology and Art," *The Swans*, ed. Peter Scott, The Wildfowl Trust, Michael Joseph, Ltd., 1972.

Feduccia, Alan: *The Age of Birds,* Harvard Univ. Press, 1980.

Forbush, Edward Howe: *Birds of America*, ed. by T. Gilbert Pason, Garden City Books, 1936.

Forbush, Edward Howe: *Natural History of Birds of Eastern and Central North America*, Houghton Mifflin Co., 1939.

Ford, Alice, ed.: *Audubon, by Himself*, American Museum of Natural History Press, 1969.

Ford, Alice: *John James Audubon*, Univ. of Oklahoma Press, 1965.

Fox, William Sherwood: *Greek and Roman Myth*, Vol. I, *Mythology of All Races*, 1916.

Frink, Maurice: "Introduction" to *Pawnee Hero Stories and Folktales* by George Bird Grinnell, Univ. of Nebraska Press, 1961.

Frye, Northrop: *Fools of Time*, Univ. of Toronto Press, 1985.

Frye, Northrop: *Words with Power*, Harcourt Brace Jovanovich Publishers, 1990.

Fuller, Errol: *Extinct Birds*, Facts on File Publications, 1988.

Gelston, W. L. and Wood, R. D.: *The Mute Swan in Northern Michigan*, 1982.

Gilliard, E. Thomas: *Living Birds of the World*, Doubleday and Co., 1958.

Godden, Rumer and Jon: "Foreword," *Mercy, Pity, Peace and Love*, Wm. Morrow, 1989.

Goodall, Jane: *My Life With the Chimpanzees*, Pocket Books, 1988.

Gooders, John: *Collins British Birds*, Wm. Collins, Sons and Co., 1982.

Gould, Stephen Jay: "Glow, Big Glowworm," *Bully for Brontosaurus*, W. W. Norton and Co., 1991.

Graham, Frank: *The Audubon Ark: A History of the National Audubon Society*, Alfred A. Knopf, 1990.

Graves, Robert: *The White Goddess*, Farrar, Strauss and Giroux, 1970.

Gray, Elizabeth Dodson: "Adam's World," produced by National Film Board of Canada, 1989.

Greenwall, Guy A.: *First Breedings of Wild Waterfowl in North America*, International Wild Waterfowl Association, Inc., 1988.

Greenway, James C., Jr.: *Extinct and Vanishing Birds of the World*, Dover Publications, Inc., 1967.

Grinnell, George Bird: *Pawnee Hero*

Stories and Folktales, Univ. of Nebraska Press, 1986.

Grimm's Fairy Tales, Transl. by Margaret Hunt, Pantheon, 1944.

Grossi, Ralph E.: "American Farmland Trust 1992 National Survey," American Farmland Trust, 1992.

Gruber, Howard: "Darwin," *Psychological Study of Scientific Creativity*, Dutton, 1991.

Gunn, W. W. H.: "Whistling Swan," *Hinterland Who's Who Series*, Canadian Wildlife Service, 1979.

Halle, Louis J.: *The Appreciation of Birds*, Johns Hopkins Univ. Press, 1989.

Hansen, Skylar: *The Trumpeter Swan: A White Perfection*, Western Horizons, 1984.

Hartwig, Dr. G.: *The Polar and Tropical Worlds*, C. A. Nichols, 1877.

Hayes, Leland B.: "Black Swans," *Gamebird Breeders, Aviculturists and Conservationists Gazette*, Oct/Nov. 1989.

Hillprecht, Albert: *Hockerschwan, Singschwan, Zwergschwan*, A. Ziemser, Verlag, 1956.

Hogben, Lancelot: *The Vocabulary of Science*, Stein and Day, 1970.

Hoagland, Kathleen, ed.: *1000 Years of Irish Poetry*, Devin-Adair Co., 1975.

Holmberg, Uno: *Siberian Mythology,* in *Mythology of all Races*, Archaeological Inst. of America, 1927.

Howard, Richard: "*Cygnus Cygnus* to Leda," *Lining Up*, Atheneum, 1985.

Hyde, Dayton O.: *Don Coyote*, Ballantine Books, 1989.

Huxley, Elspeth: *Scott of the Antarctic*, Antheneum, 1978.

Hvass, Hans: *Birds of the World*, E. P. Dutton, 1964.

Jaffe, Anielia: "Symbolism in the Visual Arts," *Man and His Symbols*, ed. Carl Jung, Dell Publ., 1968.

Johnsgard, P. A.: *Handbook of Waterfowl Behavior*, Indiana Univ. Press, 1965.

Johnsgard, P. A.: *Waterfowl of North America*, Indiana Univ. Press, 1975.

Joyce, James: *A Portrait of the Artist as a Young Man*, Viking Critical Edition, 1975.

Jung, Carl: *Man and His Symbols*, Dell Publ., 1968.

Kastner, Joseph: *A World of Watchers*, Sierra Books, 1986.

Kear, Janet: *Man and Wildfowl*, T. and A. D. Poyser, Ltd., 1990.

Kear, Janet: *The Mute Swan*, No. 27 in the Shire Natural History Series, 1988.

King, James G.: "Restoration of the Trumpeter Swan," *Newsletter*, International Wild Waterfowl Assoc., 1988.

Kortright, Francis H.: *The Ducks, Geese and Swans of North America*, Stackpole Co. and Wildlife Management Inst., 1962.

LaFlesche, F.: "War Ceremony, and Peace Ceremony of the Osage Indian," *Bulletin of the Bureau of American Ethnology,* Smithsonian Institution, 1939.

Layfield, Julianna: "The Swans of Riverbanks," *Riverbanks*, Riverbanks Zoo, Mar/April 1987.

Leopold, Aldo: *A Sand County Almanac*, Oxford Univ. Press, 1949.

Leopold, Aldo: *The River of the Mother of God*, Univ. of Wisconsin Press, 1991.

Lincoln, Frederick C.: *The Migration of Birds*, Circular 16, U.S. Fish and Wildlife, 1950.

Longfellow, Henry Wadsworth: *Song of Hiawatha*, Houghton Mifflin Co., 1901.

Lopez, Barry: *Arctic Dreams*, Bantam Edition, Bantam Books, 1987.

McCulloch, John Arnott: *Eddic*, Vol. II, *Mythology of all Races*, Archaeological Institute of America, 1930.

McKee, Russell: "Swan Shift," *Michigan Natural Resources Magazine*, July/Aug. 1984.

McKelvey, R. W.: "Trumpeter Swan," Canadian Wildlife Service, 1984.

Martin, Brian: *World Birds*, Guinness Superlatives, 1987.

Matthis, Cleopatra: "A Seasonal Record," *The Center for Cold Weather*, Sheep Meadow Press, 1989.

Matteson, Sumner and Scott Craven: *Trumpeter Swan*, Wisconsin Department of Natural Resources, 1990.

Mercante, Anthony S.: *Zoo of the Gods*, Harper and Row, 1974.

Mills, Judy: "The Swan that Would Not Fly," *National Wildlife*, National Wildlife Federation, Oct/Nov 1991.

Mighetto, Lisa: *Wild Animals and American Environmental Ethics*, University of Arizona Press, 1992.

Mountfort, Guy: *Vanished and Vanishing Birds*, Hamlyn Publ., 1985.

Moynihan, Michael: "The Swans of Abbotsbury," *The National Geographic Magazine*, Oct. 1959.

Murphy, Richard: *The Mirror Wall*, Wake Forest University Press, 1989.

Nielsen, John: "What Ever Happened to the Population Bomb?" *National Wildlife*, National Wildlife Federation, April/May 1990.

Nova, "The Mystery of Animal Pathfinders," WGBH, transcript, 1986.

Nugent, Rory: *The Search for the Pink-Headed Duck*, Houghton Mifflin, 1991.

Oliver, W. R. B.: *New Zealand Birds*, Reed, 1955.

Owen, Myrfyn and Janet Kear: "Food and Feeding Habits," *The Swans*, Peter Scott and the Wildfowl Trust, Houghton Mifflin, 1972.

Owens, Lily, ed., *The Complete Hans Christian Andersen*, Avenel Books. N.D.

Parker, Eric: *Game Birds, Beasts and Fishes*, The Lonsdale Library, Vol. XX, ed by the Earl of Lonsdale and Eric Parker, Seeley Service Co., Ltd. N.D.

Pastan, Linda: "The Keeper" *Special Report*, Whittle Communications, 1990.

Peattie, Donald Culross, ed., *Audubon's America*, Houghton Mifflin, 1940.

Peterson, Roger Tory and Virginia Marie Peterson: *Audubon's Birds of America*, Artabras Press, 1981.

Pirelli; *La Guia de Rutas, Pueblos, Ciudades y Caminos*, Pirelli, 1989.

Pinney, Roy: *The Animals in the Bible*, Chilton Books, 1964.

Press, Leslie: *Koonaworra, The Black Swan*, John Sands Ltd., 1970.

Purdy, Al: "Lament for the Dorsets," *arts canada*, Dec. 1971/Jan. 1972.

Quammen, David: *Natural Acts*, Dell Publ. Co., 1986.

Ripley, S. Dillon: *A Paddling of Ducks*, Smithsonian Institution Press, 1957.

Rothenberg, Jerome, ed.: "Magic Words," *Shaking the Pumpkin: Traditional Poetry of the Indian North Americas*, Doubleday and Co., 1972.

Rothschild, Miriam: "Introduction," *Extinct Birds*, ed. by Errol Fuller, Facts on File Publications, 1988.

Ruehrwein, Dick: "Dream Time Story," *Activity Book*, Detroit Zoo, 1989.

Ruppell, Georg: *Bird Flight*, Van Norstrand, Reinhold Co., 1977.

Sanders, Scott Russell, ed.: *Audubon Reader*, Indiana University Press, 1986.

Sass, Lorna J.: *To the King's Taste*, Metropolitan Museum of Art, 1975.

Scott, Dafila: "Swans *Semper Fidelis*," *Natural History*, July 1992.

Scott, Peter and Philippa Scott: *The Swans Fly In*, Wildfowl and Wetlands Trust, 1989.

Scott, Peter and The Wildfowl Trust, eds.: *The Swans*, Houghton Mifflin, 1972.

Scott, Peter: *Wild Chorus,* Country Life, 1939.

Scott, Peter: *A Coloured Key to the Wildfowl of the World*, The Wildfowl Trust, 1988.

Scott, Peter: *Observations of Wildlife*, Phaidon Books, Cornell Univ. Press, 1980.

Schoolcraft, Henry Rowe: "Algic Researches" in the *Song of Hiawatha* by H. W. Longfellow, Houghton Mifflin Co., 1901.

Shackleton, Keith: "Address on the Death of Sir Peter Scott," *Wildfowl and Wetlands*, May 1990.

Shea, Ruth, quoted by Todd Wilkinson in "Call of the Trumpeter," *National Parks*, July/Aug. 1991.

Sheldon, Margaret E. Thompson: "The Trumpeter's Last Call," *Nature Magazine*, Vol. 14, No. 1, July 1929.

Shorger, A. W.: *The Passenger Pigeon*, Univ. of Oklahoma Press, 1955.

Simpson, Ken and Nicolas Day: *The Birds of Australia*, Tanager Books, 1984.

Sladen, Wm. J. L.: "The Swans of Airlie," Swan Research Program at Airlie, Va., 1992.

Soothill, Eric and Whitehead, Peter: *Wildfowl of the World*, Blandford Press, 1988.

Stefferud, Alfred, ed.: *Birds in Our Lives*, U.S. Dept. of the Interior, Bureau of Sport Fisheries and Wildlife, Fish and Wildlife Serv., 1960.

Stewart, Daryl: *From the Edge of Extinction*, McClelland and Stewart, Ltd., 1979.

Stromberg, Loyl: *Swan Breeding and Management*, Stromberg Publishing Co., 1986.

Teale, Edwin Way: Audubon's Wildlife: *A New Look at Birds and Animals*, Viking Press, 1964.

Terborgh, John: *Where Have All the Birds Gone?*, Princeton Univ. Press, 1989.

Ticehurst, N.F.: *The Swan Marks of Lincolnshire*, Reprinted from the Associated Architectural and Archeological Societies' Reports and Papers, Vol. 42, 1934.

Todd, Frank: *Waterfowl*, Sea World Press, 1979.

VanDeusen, Roswell: "Mute Swan," in *Swan Breeding and Management*, Stromberg Publishing, 1986.

Van Wormer, Joe: *The World of the Swan*, J. B. Lippincott, Co., 1972.

Wallace, George J.: *An Introduction to Ornithology*, The MacMillan Co., 1957.